PEACE AND DIALOGUE IN A PLURAL SOCIETY

Contributions of the Hizmet Movement at a Time of Global Tensions

Thomas Michel

BLUE DOME

New York

Published by Blue Dome Press
244 5th Avenue, Suite D-149
New York, NY 10001, USA

www.bluedomepress.com

Library of Congress Cataloging-in-Publication Data Available

ISBN: 978-1-935295-59-4

Printed by
Imak Ofset, Istanbul - Turkey

PEACE AND DIALOGUE IN A PLURAL SOCIETY

Contents

Preface

I was pleased to learn that some Turkish friends had decided to bring together various articles and papers that I had written on Mr. M. Fethullah Gülen and to publish them in book form. This is a good initiative and one that I heartily encourage.

Although I cannot claim to more than a brief acquaintance with Mr. Gülen, or Hocaefendi ("hodjaeffendi") as he is affectionately called by those in the religious and educational movement associated with his name, I have had the opportunity to come to know personally many of the members of the movement and to witness the schools and other works carried out by the Gülen community.

In my opinion, the community is one of the most dynamic movements taking place in the Islamic *umma* at the present time. Its dynamism can be seen not only in the rapid growth of the Hizmet Movement and its diffusion beyond the geographical and social confines of Turkey, but is also evident in the number and variety of creative activities taken up by its members. New faith-based initiatives of dialogue societies, television stations, cultural tourism, specialist journals, and academic congresses, of which new examples seem to be appearing every month, have taken the community far beyond its beginnings as a student movement in İzmir, Turkey, in the 1970s. In all this activity, there is no denying the community's dynamic commitment to perform service for the general good of society.

The Hizmet Movement is playing an important role as well of cultural mediation between the international Muslim community and the non-Muslim world. Our world is still plagued by many prejudices and stereotypes which cause much misunderstanding and harm. At a time in history when Muslims are too often living with the reputation of being backward, violent and xenophobic, it is vital that the Islamic community produce, from its own spiritual resources, individuals and movements that are representative of what is finest in Islamic ideals and teaching, communities that are progressive and modern, peace-loving and open-minded, and simultaneously self-confident and respectful of others. This is the image that the Gülen community is bearing among the followers of other religions with whom they live and work.

Where did these ideas come from? The Hizmet Movement has a predecessor or spiritual mentor in the late Said Nursi, who died in 1960. This scholar, the author of the voluminous Qur'an commentary, the *Risale-i Nur*, saw the crises facing the modern world as boiling down to three. The real enemies of humankind, he stated, are three: ignorance, poverty, and disunity. Muslims delude themselves if they think that their enemies are this or that group of non-Muslims. Rather, the real need today is for people of religious commitment to be united in facing together the dangers of the time, expressed by this unholy triad of ignorance, poverty, and disunity.

It was the genius of Gülen to take up the challenge of Said Nursi to confront these enemies of modern man and to inspire, through his colleagues and disciples, concrete responses. To confront ignorance, he started student hostels and dormitories and motivated like-minded people to open schools. To confront poverty, there are the community's development programs, the communications network, and the social initiatives. To confront disunity, the Gülen community has started up an extensive network of dialogue platforms and societies aimed at building friendships and overcoming suspicions. Several of the articles in this book seek to explore the relationship between the thought of Said Nursi and the activism of Fethullah Gülen.

As I mentioned at the beginning of this Preface, I have not had the opportunity to spend much time with Mr. Gülen. I met him briefly first in İstanbul during an international congress on the *Risale-i Nur*, and then again in November 2005, when I visited his current residence in Bethlehem, Pennsylvania, U.S.A. I was part of a delegation of about 20 persons. After a simple meal, we gathered in the living room and exchanged news about recent conferences and other activities.

The next morning, after the Muslims performed the dawn prayers, they gathered again, under the guidance of Gülen, for a lengthy instruction on the Qur'an. I mention this fact, because one will miss the significance of the movement if it is not understood, first of all, as a spiritual community whose direction and strength comes from serious attention to and meditation upon the Qur'an. Gülen's role in this process is that of "teacher," which is the meaning of the title "Hoca" by which he is addressed.

This does not mean that the Hizmet Movement is a Sufi order, although there are some spiritual affinities between the thought of Said Nursi and Fethullah Gülen, on the one hand, and the traditional Sufi Masters, on the other. Some of my contributions in this book try to explore the spirituality of the movement, noting some similarities, as well as pointing out differences that distinguish the movement from traditional Sufi *tariqahs*.

What perhaps impresses outsiders the most about the movement is its openness to dialogue and cooperation with non-Muslims. For example, the movement was prominently represented at the Parliament of the World's Religions held in Capetown and Barcelona. Its dialogue societies, that the community has set up with non-Muslim collaborators in countries as disparate as Australia, Czech Republic, Austria, and U.S.A., are among the most active local proponents of interreligious dialogue today.

In recent years, the community in a number of places has undertaken projects of cultural tourism, in which Gülen community members accompany non-Muslims to Turkey on visits that combine exposure to art, history, and natural beauty with the opportunity to come to know the ideas and habits of Turkish Muslims and to build international friendships. Thus, the community has responded to a need often expressed in the tourist industry that travel to a new country ideally should not be limited to monuments and beaches, but should provide the occasion for an encounter with the people of the country visited.

For over 30 years now, Gülen's teaching has helped form many young Turkish activists. What kind of Muslims is he seeking to form? In answer, one might say, "civilized believers." Gülen's contribution to the dialogue of civilizations might be summed up in the following statement, taken from one of Gülen's recent books: "Civilization does not mean being rich and putting on fine airs, nor does it mean satisfying carnal desires and leading a luxurious, dissipated life. What it really means is being civil and courteous, kind-hearted, profound in thought, and respectful to others."[1]

Gülen's Invitation to Dialogue

The need for dialogue among people of faith has been underscored by the events of the past few years. Interreligious dialogue is seen as an alternative to the much-discussed "clash of civilizations." Those who do not subscribe to the theory that a civilizational clash is inevitable are proposing instead a dialogue of civilizations, an exchange of views aimed at mutual enrichment, a sharing of insights that can lead all to a deeper understanding of the nature of God and God's will for humankind on this planet.

That is what this book is about. It presents the thoughts of one of the most influential Muslim scholars and spiritual leaders in the Islamic world today. The movement inspired and guided by Fethullah Gülen is offering Muslims a way to live out Islamic values amidst the complex demands of modern societies. From its origins in Turkey, the movement has spread rapidly, through its schools in many countries, through its cultural and media activities, and through the social projects and dialogue encounters of Turks in diaspora in Europe, North America, and Australia, to the point that the influence of the Hizmet Movement is being felt in virtually all regions where Muslims live as majorities or minorities.

---

[1] Fethullah Gülen, *Advocate of Dialogue*, 90.

This book has a double purpose. On the one hand, it is a call to Muslims to a greater awareness that Islam teaches the need for dialogue and that Muslims are called to be agents and witnesses to God's universal mercy. Mr. Gülen calls upon his broad knowledge of the Islamic tradition by bringing together the Qur'anic Scripture, the *hadith* reports from Muhammad, and the insights of Muslims down through the ages, to build a convincing argument that tolerance, love, and compassion are genuinely Islamic values that Muslims have a duty to bring to the modern world.

On the other hand, the book is an invitation to non-Muslims to move beyond prejudice, suspicion, and half-truths in order to arrive at an understanding what Islam is really about. Someone whose knowledge of Islam is limited to the headlines of the daily newspapers is likely to believe that the religion teaches terrorism, suicide attacks, oppression of women, and hatred for those outside its community. Who would ever want to be in dialogue with people who promote such actions? Who would ever want to live among people with such attitudes?

However, through the writings of Fethullah Gülen, the reader of this book will see that a proper interpretation of Islamic teaching leads rather to truly spiritual values like forgiveness, inner peace, social harmony, honesty, and trust in God. In expressing these Islamic values, which are shared by many religious believers of various faiths, the author is not only calling Muslims to engage in dialogue, but is engaging the non-Muslim in a discussion of commonly held ideals.

I can cite my own case as an example. I am a Catholic priest, an American, who lived and worked in Rome for many years. I have known the members of the movement associated with Fethullah Gülen for almost twenty years, and I can state that they are sincerely and impressively living the teachings of their spiritual guide. They respectfully call Mr. Gülen "Hocaefendi," which simply means "Respected Teacher." The lessons in this book, derived from the Qur'an and Islamic tradition, form and shape the attitudes by which these Muslims practice their Islamic commitment. In bringing together his writings which had appeared in a wide variety of journals and interviews, many of which have never previously appeared in English, Mr. Gülen has done a good service for those who wish to know the ideals that characterize this movement.

I was delivering lectures in Urfa and Gaziantep in eastern Turkey, in 2001. I was invited to address, on my way back to Rome, a group of young people in İstanbul at a gathering organized by the Hizmet Movement. On arriving, I discovered to my surprise an assembly of perhaps 4,000 youths. In speaking with them, I found that they represented a cross section of İstanbul youth, some university students in engineering, medicine, and computer science, others working men and women. Several of the women were employed as secretaries, travel agents, or schoolteachers. I met young men who worked as bank clerks, drivers of delivery trucks, and in construction.

They were happy, enthusiastic young people who had come together to celebrate the birthday of their prophet Muhammad. It is significant that I, a Catholic priest, was invited to address them on the theme of "The Prophets, a Blessing for Humankind." My talk was followed by poetry readings in honor of Muhammad, and the evening concluded with a well-known Turkish folk singer singing hymns of praise to God accompanied by electric guitar. My feelings that evening, as on many other occasions, were that if Fethullah Gülen and his movement have been able to instill in so many young people the desire to praise and thank God and to live with love and respect for others, they must be engaged in a very valuable spiritual enterprise.

Non-Muslim believers will agree that these are people with whom we can live and cooperate for the benefit of all, but will undoubtedly ask about the views of Gülen and the movement toward others in the Muslim world who are prone to violence.

I conclude this Preface by citing a passage that sums up Gülen's approach as a spiritual teacher:

> If I had the ability to read people's minds, that is, if I had the ability to know everyone with his/her particular characteristics, I would direct each person to the hill of perfection that is

the most appropriate for him/her. I would recommend continuous reflection, contemplation, reading; I would tell them
to study the signs of God in the universe and in people themselves; I would advise people to busy themselves with the
study of the Qur'an; I would advise others to recite a portion
of the Qur'an and certain prayers on a regular basis; I would
tell still others to continuously reflect on "natural" phenomena. That is, I would designate duties for people in the areas
in which they have natural abilities.[2]

I want to alert the reader to the fact that the various chapters in this book were originally papers delivered at academic
conferences or talks given to various audiences around the
world. As a result the reader will find some repetition, especially
in the factual information, if not in the analytical passages. I
apologize for this and hope that this will not provide too much of
a distraction. Rather than being a scientific study of the thought
of Fethullah Gülen and the growth of the Hizmet Movement, the
chapters of this book are to be seen as the personal reflections of
a sympathetic observer and an ongoing dialogue partner. After
two decades of study and interaction, I remain in deep admiration for the ideas and projects of Mr. Gülen and the many friends
I have come to know through the movement.

Thomas Michel, S.J.

---

2   Fethullah Gülen, *Advocate of Dialogue*, Fairfax, VA: The Fountain, 2000,
    p. 90

PART ONE

On Fethullah Gülen

A Sufi-Type Spirituality
for Modern Societies

The Need for a Modern Spirituality

The emergence in Europe and North America of interest in the thought of Turkish scholar Fethullah Gülen is a phenomenon that demands explanation. Several American universities, such as Rice and Georgetown, have held academic seminars to study the various aspects of his thought. In Europe, in the Netherlands, for example, at least four universities (Nijmegen, Tilburg, Erasmus in Rotterdam, and Amsterdam) have hosted seminars on "Forerunners for Peace," which prominently feature the views of Gülen and his movement.

In trying to understanding the reasons for this, I think that several factors can be mentioned. Firstly, people who feel oppressed by the materialist and consumerist character of modern life are looking for a spirituality that can point a way to live authentically and usefully, and many find such a spirituality in the writings and movement of Fethullah Gülen. Secondly, Muslims seeking a way to live their Islamic faith in modern situations and make a positive contribution to the transformation of society find in the movement a constructive interpretation of Qur'anic teaching that stresses good deeds and service to humanity. Thirdly, non-Muslims who are looking for Muslim partners with whom they can live and work together, share ideas, and form friendships find in the Hizmet Movement a body of ethically concerned individuals who are open to cooperate in a pluralist approach to issues of peace, justice, and human development. All these factors contribute to the interest in the ideas of Mr. Gülen and the activities of the movement associated with his name shown in universities, community centers, churches and mosques.

In my paper, I cannot hope to treat all aspects of the thought of Fethullah Gülen or all the activities of the movement associated with his name. I intend to take up only one aspect, that is the Sufi-oriented spirituality of Gülen's interpretation of Islamic life and teaching.

A recent survey of people under the age of 30 in Europe showed that there is a decreasing interest in "religion," but a corresponding increase of interest in "spirituality." At first glance, this seems inconsistent, but it does reflect, I believe, a widespread and typical modern attitude. When people express disinterest in "religion," I believe that they are referring to traditional ritual, which they consider, perhaps based on their own unhappy experience, to be dry, formalistic, and empty of deeper meaning. Conversely, their interest in spirituality reflects the need for some form of contact with the Divine in their lives. They are dissatisfied with a purely positivist approach to life and are seeking transcendent input, relevant insights which can help them deal with the challenges raised by post-modern living, a program of exercises that can help one progress on the path of personal interior growth and transformation.

Sufism, the generally accepted term for the Islamic mystical tradition, is seen by many as offering such food for the spirit. Sufism is not a single clearly defined movement, but an interrelated network of ideas and practices aimed at a deeper understanding and faithful pursuit of the Qur'anic message. Non-Muslim scholars,[3] as well as Sufis themselves,[4] who attempt to give a succinct definition of Sufism inevitably pull out certain elements and emphases that have been central among some Sufis at various periods of history, while disregarding or glossing over other characteristics that do not fit in and perhaps even contradict their definition.

For some, it is *asceticism* and simplicity of life that is the key to a true following of Islam. Others emphasize *love* as the central idea and understand the Sufi path as one leading to a union of love with God, the Beloved. For others, Sufism is a voluntarist path by which the believer, by concentrating on virtue and moral behavior, comes into a union of *will* with God, a state in which the mystic no longer has an independent will of his or her own, but seeks only to do the will of God. Many mystics see the Path as primarily one of *knowledge*, of becoming aware of the eternal Truth, the perennial wisdom of the heart that is the only sure font of true insight. Still others affirm the *oneness of all existence*, so that the mystical path is essentially a *psychological* movement toward awareness that the believer is simply a transient manifestation of the eternal One present in the cosmos and at the depths of one's own personality. Some Sufis emphasize extraordinary mystical *experience*, expressed in states of ecstasy, inspired utterances, visions, and dreams, while for others the path is a contemplative *pilgrimage* to God residing in the silent cave of the heart.

---

3 Anne-Marie Schimmel, in her treatment "What is Sufism?" never attempts a comprehensive definition, but rather cites the partial description of Sufism given my many Sufis and scholars (*Mystical Dimensions of Islam*, 3-22).

4 Ruwaym's description comes perhaps the closest: "The Sufis are people who prefer God to everything and God prefers them to everything else" (Cited in Schimmel, 15).

Fethullah Gülen and Sufism

When one studies the writings and the actions of Fethullah Gülen in this context, the first question to be asked is whether he is a Sufi. At various times in his life, Mr. Gülen has had to defend his movement from accusations that he has founded a new Sufi order, of which he is regarded as the *shaykh*.[5] In Turkey today, the charge of founding a secret *tariqah* (*tarikat* in Turkish) carries legal and political implications. Secular modernists view Sufism as part of the pre-modern past, a relic from Ottoman times, an obstacle to progress, development and prosperity. Conversely, Muslim activists of *salafi* tendency view Sufism as responsible for introducing unwarranted and unorthodox innovations and for promulgating a passive, pietistic religiosity.

In response, Gülen affirms that he has not founded a *tariqah* and moreover, that he has never belonged to any Sufi order. He states: "The religious orders are institutions that appeared six centuries after our Prophet, upon whom be peace, in the name of representing Sufism. They have their own rules and structures. Just as I never joined a Sufi order, I have never had any relationship with one."[6] To the question of why he is called *Hoca*, literally, "Teacher," a form of address traditionally used by Sufis for their master, he answers that the title carries no hierarchical or Ottoman revivalist connotation, but is simply "a respectful way of addressing someone whose knowledge on religious matters is recognized and acknowledged by the general public."[7]

Given that Gülen has never belonged to a *tariqah*, is it still accurate to regard him as a Sufi? In a seminal work[8] on Sufi ele-

---

5   Thomas Michel, "Fethullah Gülen as Educator," 83.
6   Fethullah Gülen, cited in L. E. Webb, *Fethullah Gülen: Is There More to Him than Meets the Eye*, 103.
7   Ibid., 80.
8   Zeki Saritoprak, "Fethullah Gülen: A Sufi in His Own Way," 156-169. Saritoprak's paper is the first to study the Sufi elements in Gülen's thought; I will try not to repeat what he has stated.

ments in Gülen's thought, Zeki Saritoprak calls Gülen "a Sufi in his own way."[9] Saritoprak affirms that many Sufis belonged to no Sufi Order. For the first six centuries of Islam, there were no Sufi Orders, yet there were many important Sufis. Even after the appearance of Sufi orders in the 13th and 14th Century, there are instances of well-known Sufis who did not belong to any *tariqah*.

Yet the appearance of the "independent Sufi" has usually been considered anomalous by most practitioners of the Sufi path. Saritoprak notes the problematic situation of the modern Sufi who follows no *tariqah* and has no spiritual guide.

"Early Sufis had neither orders nor even Sufi organizations. Rabia, Junayd, Muhasibi, Bishr, Ghazzali, Fariduddin Attar, and even Rumi did not belong to a *tariqah*. However, they were Sufis. From the vantage point of institutionalized Sufism, their Sufism would be problematic, because these early Sufis did not have a spiritual master. In the Sufi tradition, he who has no a *shaykh*, finds Satan as his *shaykh*.[10]

Concerning the necessity for a spiritual guide, it is true that the vast majority of Sufis have discouraged or even forbidden one from following the Sufi path without a *shaykh* or *pir*. However, a minority view has always held that the spiritual guide need not be a living person. Kharaqani, for example, was initiated into the Sufi path by the spirit of Abu Yazid al-Bistami, while 'Attar was inspired by the spirit of Al-Hallaj. Other Sufis claimed to have as their guide Khidr, the mysterious companion of Moses whose story is recounted in the Qur'an.

---

9 Yılmaz supports this view. "Most scholars agree that 'Gülen continues a long Sufi tradition of seeking to address the spiritual needs of people, to educate the masses, and to provide some stability in times of turmoil'." İhsan Yılmaz, citing Ebru Altınoğlu, "Fethullah Gülen's Perception of State and Society," 102, in "*Ijtihad* and *Tajdid* by Conduct: The Gülen Movement," 228.

10 Ibid., 160.

Gülen's position is that he is guided in his spiritual development by the Qur'an and the Sunna. In Gülen's view, the Qur'an is
not only the best guide, but is the source and font of all Sufi
thought and practice. Rooted in the Qur'an and Sunna, and sup-
plemented by the views and experiences of later Sufis down
through the centuries who applied the Qur'anic teachings through
their own personal efforts (*ijtihad*), Sufism must not be considered an "alternative" path followed by some Muslims in contra-
distinction or in contradiction to the *sharia*, but rather, Sufism
should be regarded as one of the basic sciences of Islam.

> [*Tasawwuf*] is not contradictory with any of the Islamic ways
> based on the Book and the *Sunna*. Far from being contradic-
> tory, it has its source, just like the other religious sciences, in
> the Book and the *Sunna* and the conclusions the purified
> scholars of the early period of Islam drawn from the Qur'an
> and the *Sunna—ijtihad*.[11]

For Gülen, *tasawwuf* and *sharia* are two aspects of the same
truth or, one could say, two ways of expressing the same truth.
The two forms of expression arise from differences in personal-
ity rather than from any contradictory messages. Both lead the
Muslim to believe and practice the one Islamic truth, but each
Muslim must find the path most suited to his disposition.

> While adherence to the former [*sharia*] has been regarded as
> exotericism (self-restriction to the outward dimension of reli-
> gion), following the latter [*tasawwuf*] has been seen as pure
> esotericism. Although this discrimination partly arises from
> the assertions that the commandments of Sharia are repre-
> sented by jurisprudents or muftis, and the other by the Sufis, it
> should be viewed as the result of a natural human tendency,
> which is that everyone gives priority to the way more compat-
> ible with his temperament and for which he has aptitude.[12]

---

[11] Fethullah Gülen, *Key Concepts in the Practice of Sufism*, 9.
[12] Ibid., 7.

Sufism has known antinomian (*bi-shara*) Sufis who claimed that following the exoteric (*zahir*) regulations of the *sharia* were unnecessary for those on the esoteric (*batin*) path, but Gülen's position comes down clearly in the *ba-shara* camp of those who stress the importance for the Sufi to not abandon the *sharia*. Gülen exemplifies the long line of *sharia*-oriented Sufis, represented most strongly by the Qadiri and Naqshbandi traditions, and in modern times by Said Nursi, who regard *tasawwuf* as an interiorized facet of the life of the sincere Muslim who seeks to live fully the message contained in the Qur'an and Sunna.

Ozdalga sees three "positive reference points" which have shaped Gülen's thinking: 1) orthodox Sunni Islam, 2) the Naqshbandi Sufi tradition, 3) the Nurculuk movement, that is, those Muslims influenced by the writings of Said Nursi.[13] The Naqshbandis have always insisted on the careful performance of the prescriptions of the *sharia*, so there is no contradiction between the first two points. Gülen differs from the Naqshbandi Order, however, in that the Naqshbandi disciple is presented with an explicit program of spiritual development, which is closely monitored by the *shaykh*, whereas Gülen's approach is more open-ended in stressing good deeds and service to humanity (*hizmet*) more than spiritual exercises and devotions.

Probably the most important formative influence on the development of Gülen's thought, including his approach to Sufism, was Said Nursi.[14] Like Nursi, who was also formed in the Naqshbandi tradition but chose to work and teach outside the confines of an established *tariqah*, so also Gülen sees the Sufi tradition more as the accumulated wisdom of the saints of Islam, rather than an institutionalized necessity for achieving the internaliza-

---

13 Elisabeth Özdalga, "Worldly Asceticism in Islamic Casting: Fethullah Gülen's Inspired Piety and Activism," 91.

14 In his commentary on Nursi's *Al-Mathnawi al-Nuriya* (The Epitomes of Light), Gülen refers to Said Nursi as "the Master" and urges that his works be studied in depth.

tion of Islamic values. According to Nursi, Sufism "has been pro-claimed, taught, and described in thousands of books written by the scholars among the people of illumination and those who have had unfolded to them the reality of creation, who have told the Muslim community and us of that truth."[15]

Moreover, like Said Nursi, Gülen is aware that not everything that historically has passed in the name of Sufism is of positive value. A critical approach to the Sufi tradition, however, must recognize the intrinsic strength of the movement as an instrument for fostering and building a sense of community and brotherhood. As Said Nursi states:

> The Sufi path may not be condemned because of the evils of certain ways which have adopted practices outside the bounds of *taqwa*, and even of Islam, and have wrongfully given themselves the name of Sufi paths. Quite apart from the important and elevated religious and spiritual results of the Sufi path and those that look to the hereafter, it is the Sufi paths which are the first and most effective and fervent means of expanding and developing brotherhood, a sacred bond within the World of Islam.[16]

Gülen understands Sufism as the inner dimension of the *sharia*, and the two dimensions must never be separated. Performance of the externals without attention to their interior transformative power results in dry ritualism. Concentration on the interior disciplines and rejecting prescribed ritual and behavior reduces spiritual striving to following one's own preferences and proclivities. Only by activating both dimensions of Islam will the seeker be able to humbly submit (*islam*) one's life fully to God.

---

[15] Said Nursi, *The Letters* (The Twenty-ninth Letter, Ninth Section, First Allusion), 518.

[16] Said Nursi, *The Letters* (Twenty-ninth Letter, Ninth Section, Third Allusion), 521.

An initiate or traveler on the path (*salik*) never separates the outer observance of the Sharia from its inner dimension, and therefore observes all of the requirements of both the outer and the inner dimensions of Islam. Through such observance, he or she travels toward the goal in utmost humility and submission.[17]

Just as Sufism is what "brings to life the religious sciences," in Al-Ghazali's phrase, so the *sharia* is what keeps the believer rooted in the Islamic tradition.

> If the traveler has not been able to prepare his heart according to both the requirements of his spiritual journeying and the commandments of the Sharia, that is, if he does not think and reason in the light of Prophethood while his feelings fly in the boundless realm of his spiritual state, he will inevitably fall. He will be confused and bewildered, speaking and acting contrary to the spirit of the Sharia.[18]

According to Saritoprak, both the appellation, the question of whether one is *called* a Sufi, as well as that of membership in a *tariqah* are secondary. He cites Mawlana Jalaluddin Rumi to the effect that it is not the external trappings that make one a Sufi but the purity of one's interior disposition:

Gülen never calls himself a Sufi. One is not a Sufi in name, but rather in spirit and heart. As Rumi says: "What makes the Sufi? Purity of heart, not the patched mantle and the perverse lust of those earth-bound men who steal his name. He [the true Sufi] in all things discerns the pure essence." In short, Gülen understands that one may annihilate himself in the rays of the existence of the Truth through knowing of his impotence, poverty and nothingness.[19]

17 Fethullah Gülen, "Sufism and Its Origins," 1999.
18 Fethullah Gülen, *Key Concepts in the Practice of Sufism*, 190.
19 Saritoprak, 168.

If Gülen is to be considered a Sufi, at least in spirit, and perhaps also in name, what does Sufism mean to him? In two works on the subject, Gülen offers his own definition. In the earlier work he states "*Tasawwuf* [Sufism] means that by being freed from the vices and weaknesses particular to human nature and acquiring angelic qualities and conduct pleasing to God, one lives one's life in accordance with the requirements of knowledge and love of God and in the spiritual delight that comes thereby."[20] In the later work, he gives a very similar definition of the Sufi path: "Sufism is the path followed by an individual who, having been able to free himself or herself from human vices and weaknesses in order to acquire angelic qualities and whose conduct is pleasing to God, lives in accordance with the requirements of God's knowledge and love and in the resulting spiritual delight that ensues."[21]

Both definitions come down to the same thing. Gülen gives priority to the will, emphasizing that Sufism means overcoming the human obstacles to God's power and grace and acquiring the virtues and behavior that God desires in His servants.[22] The person who lives in this way is gradually growing in *ma'rifa* or spiritual wisdom and in love (*mahabba*, *'ashq*), both for God and for others. God encourages and confirms the faithful follower of this path by granting the gift of spiritual joy. This understanding is consistent with the mainstream of Sufi teaching down through the centuries, in which the Sufi exerts his or her own efforts to attain the various spiritual stations (*maqamat*), thereby removing one by one the obstacles to divine grace, and then waits trustfully for God to grant as gifts the spiritual states (*ahwal*) of knowledge, love, and delight.

---

20 Fethullah Gülen, *Key Concepts*, 2.
21 Fethullah Gülen, *Key Concepts*, xiv.
22 "Such a transformation results in God's directing the individual's will in accordance with His will." Fethullah Gülen, *Toward a Global Civilization of Love and Tolerance*, 164.

What is the attraction of the Sufi tradition for Gülen? In a telling comment, he notes that the Muslims who, down through the centuries, most reflected upon and sought to practice the interior values taught by Islam and who developed the spiritual disciplines for controlling selfish impulses, were in fact Sufis. One could almost say that Sufism is the *essence* or, as he states elsewhere, the *spirit* of Islam.

> As a religion, Islam naturally emphasizes the spiritual realm. It takes the training of the ego as a basic principle. Asceticism, piety, kindness and sincerity are essential to it. In the history of Islam, the discipline that dwelt most on these matters was Sufism. Opposing this would be opposing the essence of Islam.[23]

Here Gülen finds the importance of Sufism for a modern Islamic spirituality. He sees Sufism as offering a program of discipline by which the believer can step by step renounce consumerist tendencies and a secular heedlessness. This renunciation is not seen as an empty asceticism for its own sake, but is oriented, rather, toward the greater reward of becoming aware of spiritual realities. For Gülen, as had previously been taught by Al-Ghazali, Sufism brings the blessing of an experiential confirmation of the truths of faith which has previously been only intellectually apprehended. Gülen explains:

> Sufism enables individuals to deepen their awareness of themselves as devotees of God. Through the renunciation of this transient, material world, as well as the desires and emotions it engenders, they awaken to the reality of the other world, which is turned toward God's Beautiful Names. Sufism allows individuals to develop the moral dimension of one's existence, and enables the acquisition of a strong, heartfelt, and personally experienced conviction of the articles of faith that before had only been accepted superficially.[24]

---

[23] Gülen, cited in Webb, 103.
[24] Fethullah Gülen, *Advocate of Dialogue*, 352.

In other words, the genius of Sufism, according to Gülen, is its ability to *interiorize* the message of the Qur'an and Sunna so that it influences and shapes the behavior of the Muslim. Through Sufism, the Muslim learns to move beyond obeying commands and regulations that he or she does not understand to an appreciation of Islamic teaching which becomes part and parcel of the believer's way of life. Sufism shows how a Muslim can overcome selfish tendencies, respond to frustration and opposition, and with patience and perseverance move beyond discouragement and routine. Sufism enables the Muslim to attain the virtuous qualities and the personal disciplines required to live fully in accord with the will of God. Sufism leads the way to *shawq*, delight, so that religious commitment is not some onerous and unpleasant burden that a person is forced to carry, but can be conducive to a joyful, loving acceptance of life.

What is of most interest for Gülen in Sufism is its ability to provide a practical program by which the Muslim can internalize Islamic faith so that it motivate a life of service to humankind. For Gülen, the ecstatic or para-normal mystical experiences sometimes claimed by or for Sufi saints appear to be of relatively little interest.

Gülen's appreciation for the teaching of the Sufi masters does not prevent him from criticizing occasionally the way that Sufi life was often put into practice. The dynamism of the early Sufis often got dissipated in the institutional forms that took shape in the later Sufi Orders. Particularly in recent times, many Sufis divorced themselves from real life and engaged in useless metaphysical speculation. They are one of the groups, in Gülen's view, who have been responsible for the crisis of education in the Muslim world, including the Turkish republic.

In fact, his educational efforts can be understood as a reaction to the impoverishment of choice in educational possibilities available to Turkish students. It is the lack of integration between scientific knowledge and spiritual values which led Gülen and his associates to conceive a new type of education. Until the inception of the educational project undertaken by Gülen and his colleagues, Turkish students were forced to study either at schools on the secular republican model, at traditional *madrasas*, at the Sufi *takyas*, or at military academies. None of these models was able to integrate successfully scientific training with human and spiritual values. "At a time when modern schools concentrated on ideological dogmas, institutions of religious education (*madrasas*) broke with life, institutions of spiritual training (*takyas*) were immersed in sheer metaphysics, and the army restricted itself to sheer force, this coordination [of knowledge] was essentially not possible."[25]

The Sufi *takyas*, although they had concerned themselves with fostering the development of spiritual values, have failed to meet the challenges of contemporary society and, in Gülen's word, "console themselves with virtues and wonders of the saints who had lived in previous centuries." Even if the way that Sufism was handed down in recent decades has not been able to provide guidance for the modern Muslim, a renewed approach to the Sufi tradition can enrich still Muslim spirituality and offer direction for the future. For if a key precondition for the progress of civilization is the changing of outdated and ineffective mentalities,[26] this is only achieved when someone acknowledges his own limitations, recognizes the need for controlling his impulses, and finds motivation to strive for virtue and knowledge.

This, according to Gülen, is what Sufism is all about. "The Islamic spiritual life based on asceticism, regular worship, abstention from all major and minor sins, sincerity and purity of intention, love and yearning, and the individual's admission of his essential impotence and destitution became the subject-matter of Sufism."[27]

---

25 Fethullah Gülen, *Towards the Lost Paradise*, 11.
26 Fethullah Gülen, *Towards the Lost Paradise*, 71.
27 Fethullah Gülen, *Criteria or Lights of the Way*, I, 50.

The Sufi training, as a discipline which highlights the inner dimension of Islamic teaching, enables the Muslim to confront critically but with moderation the challenges of modernity without falling into the snares either of unreflective acceptance or angry refusal. The question all modern people face is how to develop humane qualities, good behavior, love for others, enthusiasm for self-improvement, and an active desire to serve others, make a difference in the world, and to persevere in this desire in the face of setbacks and failures. For the Muslim, according to Gülen, it is the Sufi thinkers who, down through the centuries, have thought through these questions and have followed the experimental method of dealing with them.

If the modern Muslim wants to engage modernity critically and make necessary changes, he or she must begin each with one's own self. Sufism offers the collected wisdom transmitted down through the centuries by which one can proceed towards a transformed mentality, deeper love, positive character traits, and courage to work for the improvement of society.

The spiritual program offered by Sufism provides a firm basis for purifying modern scientific study from its ethical inadequacies and positivist limitations. In this way, science and humanities, scientific and humane values, a scientific and a religious approach to life, can be reconciled. This is the challenge facing scholars, educators, and communicators today.

Following in the
Footsteps of Rumi

The Greatness of Rumi

Among the medieval mystical poets, the one who speaks most clearly and directly to the modern world is Jalaluddin Rumi. In the Muslim world, he is simply known as *Mawlana*, "Our Master." Just like in St. Louis if you say "Stan the Man" or "El Hombre," everyone knows who you are talking about, so too in the Middle East if you speak of Mawlana, "Our Master," everyone recognizes that you are referring to Rumi. The depth of his spiritual experience, his original and arresting poetic images, his obvious sincerity and openheartedness, and his ability to transcend cultures, time periods, and religions, all go together to make Rumi one of the most accessible and influential of Muslim thinkers who speak to us from the past.

The number of internet web pages devoted to translations of Rumi's poetry is evidence of the extent to which Mawlana is known and loved even in the West, but this is nothing compared to his influence on modern thinkers and scholars in the Muslim world, and his place in the heart of ordinary Muslim worshiper. Rumi's poetry is known through recitations and classical performances of the poems in their musical settings; his verses are quoted in the text of popular songs and novels. I have seen verses of Rumi's poetry decorating dishes and wood panels in homes. I have even seen his verses bedecking horse carts and their modern equivalent, minibuses.

In their whirling meditation, the dervishes of the Mawlawi Sufi Order founded by Rumi communicate in a non-verbal way

Rumi's message of tolerance, peace, and deep absorption in the Divine. Accompanied by hymns of praise to God and to the prophet Muhammad, the dervishes whirl like the earth turning on its axis and they focus on the God who is at the heart and center of all. One of the most popular festivals in Turkey is the *Shab Arus*, literally, "The Wedding Night." Held every year for the past 738 years, the two-week celebration in Konya commemorates Rumi's earthly departure on 17 December 1273 and celebrates the reunion of his soul with the Divine Beloved.

In a beautiful image, Rumi invites you, the reader, to imagine yourself as a stranger in a foreign land. The night is dark and cold and you feel very much alone in this unfamiliar place. As you walk along, you eventually come to a house. Looking through the open door, you can see a well-lighted room, with people sitting in a circle on the floor around a hearth. They are eating and drinking and talking and singing, when one of the friends looks up and notices you, a stranger, at the door. He calls out Rumi's famous words of welcome:

> "Come, come, whoever you are,
> Wanderer, idolater, worshipper of fire,
> Come even though you have broken your vows a thousand times,
> Come, and come again.
> Ours is not a caravan of despair."

The message is clear: true religion is about love, it extends an invitation to anyone who is lost, searching, uprooted, or with a history of failure or betrayal to come to the light, the warmth, and the joy of a loving, welcoming community. It is ultimately about hope, the antidote to aimless drifting or anguished desperation.

Rumi's message of faith as an abode of peace and joyful fellowship has inspired many modern Muslims and others down through the centuries by means of the beautiful poetic imagery with which he expressed his spirituality. In a way similar to that of Christian mystics like John of the Cross and Teresa of Avila,

Rumi described the soul's relation to God in the imagery of human love. God is both the Beloved for whom one longs and pines and the Lover who patiently awaits the moment of our reunion.

Rumi's Influence on Fethullah Gülen

Even after eight centuries, Rumi's writings continue to influence both Muslim scholars and ordinary believers. One modern Muslim who has appropriated Rumi's insights and integrated them into his own understanding of Islamic faith and life is the Turkish scholar, Fethullah Gülen. The correspondence of Rumi to Gülen is that of kindred spirits who, across the centuries, share an interpretation of the Qur'anic message as well as a commitment to communicate that message to their contemporaries. In his sermons and written works, Gülen frequently cites Rumi's behavior and attitudes to illustrate his message; in his four-volume work on Islamic spirituality, Gülen refers to Rumi more often than to any other spiritual writer as he seeks to initiate the seeker into the mysteries of God's love.

What does Mawlana mean for Fethullah Gülen? Where does he see the affinity between his own understanding of Islam and that expounded and exemplified by Rumi? What are the lessons that can be learned from Rumi? Why does Gülen consider Rumi a worthy exemplar for the modern Muslim?

Firstly, he sees Rumi as the model of tolerance and dialogue in Islam. Almost a century ago, Said Nursi, one of the most influential Muslim scholars in modern Turkey, proposed that Muslims should be united with true Christians in bearing witness to divine values in the face of a world in which aggressive materialism was on the rise. To this end, Nursi proposed that Muslims should avoid entering into controversy with Christians. "The old way of acting is impossible. Controversial subjects should not be discussed with Christians." In commenting on this proposal, Gülen states that in this Nursi is acting in a similar manner to that of Rumi, who described himself as a compass, one foot fixed firmly in the center while the other turns in a broad arc to complete a full circle. The foot planted in the center that never changes position is the faith conviction by which one is united to God as the unmoving heart and center of one's existence, while the other foot moves freely "to embrace all believers." In other words, Gülen is proposing that his disciples be deeply rooted in their Islamic faith and at the same time reach out in dialogue in all directions to people of good will.

Gülen took Said Nursi's encouragement of Muslim-Christian unity and extended it to Jews and to the followers of other religions. In a message to the Parliament of the World's Religions in Cape Town in 1999, Gülen presented an optimistic vision of interreligious harmony: "It is my conviction that in the future years, the new millennium will witness unprecedented religious blooming and the followers of world religions, such as Muslims, Christians, Jews, Buddhists, Hindus and others, will walk hand-in-hand to build a promised bright future of the world." According to Gülen, dialogue is not merely a strategic alliance among religions to combat a materialistic world-view but, at least for Muslims, it is demanded by the nature of religion itself. As he stated in the same message: "The very nature of religion demands this dialogue. Judaism, Christianity, and Islam, and even Hinduism and Buddhism pursue the same goal. As a Muslim, I accept all Prophets and books sent to different peoples throughout history, and regard belief in them as an essential principle of being Muslim."[28]

Gülen endorses Nursi's view that the days of the use of force are over; today's methods of persuasion are those of peaceful dialogue, scientific argumentation and rational debate. In place of the "jihad of the sword" he calls for "jihad of the word." The "jihad of the word" focuses on attracting others by one's example and seeking to convince others of the truth of one's position by reasonable argumentation, never imposing one's views by

---

[28] Fethullah Gülen, Capetown, 1999, p. 14.

force. For Gülen, this mode of discussion is the only manner of confrontation suited to the true nature of Islam.

Understanding Islam to be a religion consisting of peace and tolerance, Gülen holds up the example of Rumi as foremost among those figures in Islamic history who best embody these values. Gülen calls Rumi "one of the people of love." He writes: "If one were to seek the true face of Islam in its own sources, history, and true representatives, one would discover that it is a religion of forgiveness, pardon, and tolerance, as saints and teachers of love and tolerance like Rumi, and many others have so beautifully expressed."

Gülen envisions conscientious people of faith today as facing three universal enemies. These are not the enemies of Muslims alone. They are equally the enemies of Jews, Christians, and the followers of other religions. They are enemies that we must face together if we ever hope to overcome them. These enemies are ignorance, poverty, and disunity.

To fight ignorance, Gülen has inspired his followers to open and operate schools in more than 100 countries. They have published newspapers, popular magazines, and professional journals, started television networks, and opened twelve universities. In Turkey, where I used to live, I taught English, along with many well-trained Turkish volunteers, at several of the 45 free schools for children in poor slum areas of Ankara that are run by members of their movement.

To fight poverty, those inspired by Gülen's teachings have founded a relief and development agency that now works in over 55 countries. Operating with an annual budget of $300 million dollars for the last three years,[29] they provide daily meals for 65,000 hungry people and this past Ramadan they fed over a quarter million people in soup kitchens in Asia, Africa, and the

---

29 Savaş Metin, Secretary General Kimse Yok Mu, "Turkish Biggest NGO Chief Discloses Plans to Extend to Gambia," *Daily Observer*, 28 February 2014.

Middle East. They have been digging fresh-water wells in Niger, Somalia, and Sudan's Darfur region.

To fight disunity, Gülen's followers have started dialogue and friendship centers all over the world. In the United States alone, there are about 200 of these centers. Disunity arises from people not knowing one another; consequently, they are suspicious, afraid, and think the worst of the other. To overcome this disunity, the Niagara Foundation and its sister organizations elsewhere hold friendship dinners; they organize visits to Turkey so that others can enjoy and appreciate the culture of their native land; they organize speakers' series, luncheon forums, picnics, art and food festivals, and give awards for outstanding achievements in promoting dialogue.

When we gather at a Friendship Dinner, we are like the guests invited into Rumi's community of warmth and light. We have accepted the invitation and let ourselves be part of that circle of those who long for unity and harmony, who strive to break the bonds of disunity among humankind. And we are grateful to Fethullah Gülen and his community for having extended this invitation to us. According to Gülen, Rumi and those like him are not marginal or eccentric Muslims, but they represent the mainstream of Islamic thought and practice down through the centuries. Gülen invites his followers to look to "the lovers—the people of love," as Rumi calls them, to discover and follow the example of those who have come to understand Islam as a message of love. He invites them to share with us Rumi's famous invitation:

> "Come, come and join us; we are the people of love devoted to God!
> Come, come through the door of love; join us and sit with us.
> Come, let us speak one to another through our hearts.
> Let us speak secretly, without ears and eyes.
> Let us laugh together without lips or sound, let us laugh like the roses.
> Since we are all the same, let us call each other from our hearts,
> But we won't use our lips or tongue."

Peace and Dialogue in a Plural Society: Common Values and Responsibilities

I would like to begin by congratulating the Australian Intercultural Society for organizing and holding this conference on the theme of "Peace and Dialogue in a Plural Society: Common Values and Responsibilities." This is exactly the kind of initiative that is urgently needed around the world today, as we try, through dialogue, to build communication and respect as an alternative to suspicion and violence.

Dialogue is a much used—perhaps excessively used term in our times—but for Christians and Muslims, who make up the great majority of the participants at our conference, it refers to an important task of those who believe in and worship God and seek to do God's will in our societies. Dialogue does not simply mean talking to one another, but goes beyond talking to include listening to each other, studying problems together, working together for the good of all and, most of all, living together in peace and harmony. It involves an openness to those whose religious or ethnic group is different from our own; it means accepting them as they are, without feeling that we have to change them and make them like ourselves.

The Roots of Dialogue: Catholic Church

In the Catholic Church, our commitment to engage in dialogue with Muslims goes back to the time of the Second Vatican Council in 1965. The Council is made up of the Catholic bishops from all over the world, together with the Pope, who presides over the Council, and is the most authoritative body in the Catholic Church. In one of its decrees, the document *Nostra Aetate*, the Council speaks, for the first time in history of the Catholic Church, about Muslims. It calls on Catholics to have "respect and esteem" for Muslims and lists the many grounds for which this respect is due. First and foremost is the fact that Muslims worship the One and only God, just as do Christians, and like Christians, Muslims seek to do God's will in all things. The document goes on to list prayer, almsgiving and fasting, three pillars of Islamic practice, as further reasons why Christians should respect Muslims. Finally, the statement concludes by acknowledging that in the course of history, Christians and Muslims have not always lived in peace, but have in various times and places engaged in enmity, conflict and at times even warfare. But it calls on both communities to move beyond the past to cooperate with each other in four key areas of modern life: in working for peace, liberty, social justice, and moral values.

This decree of the Second Vatican Council is important because it shows that for Catholics, having respect and esteem for Muslims is not simply the personal choice of a few individuals, an element of Christian faith which one can take or leave as one wishes, but is a part of how the Catholic Church understands what it means to be a Christian today. I should note that as a Catholic I am most knowledgeable about the roots of dialogue in the Catholic Church, there have been parallel developments in other Christian Churches, especially in the members of the World Council of Churches.

If there were no follow up, no genuine effort to build mutual understanding and cooperation with Muslims, one could claim that the statements of these Churches, like the decree Nostra Aetate, were really only a kind of public relations, similar to the way that movie stars and other public figures will kiss and profess great affection for those whom they really dislike. But we can point to a tremendous development in the years since the Second Vatican Council. Pope John Paul II met with Muslims over 60 times, more than all previous Popes put together. For 13 years I worked at the Vatican's Council for Interreligious Dialogue as Head of the Office for relations with Muslims, and I can testify that the efforts of dialogue on the part of the Catholic Church have been sincere and real.

Dialogue needs two willing partners; otherwise, one would have a monologue. I know that other speakers on this panel are far better prepared than I to explain the roots of dialogue in the Islamic tradition. I will limit myself to pointing out, mainly to my fellow Christians, that Muslims have not always been in a passive state of waiting to be invited to dialogue, but have often taken the first initiative. In Yogyakarta, Indonesia, for example, where I have lived for many years, we had a very active faith-discussion group, at the initiative of Muslim colleagues in the Islamic colleges, already some years before the Second Vatican Council.

Bediüzzaman Said Nursi: A Muslim Teacher Who Advocated Dialogue

I would like to illustrate my point by outlining the contributions to the idea and practice of Muslim-Christian dialogue made by two key individuals in recent Turkish history. Long before the Second Vatican Council, Bediüzzaman Said Nursi (1876-1960), one of the most influential Muslim thinkers of the 20th Century, advocated a dialogue between true Muslims and true Christians. The earliest statement of Said Nursi concerning the need for dialogue between Muslims and Christians dates from 1911, more than 50 years before the Council document, Nostra Aetate.

Said Nursi was led to his view about the need for Muslim-Christian dialogue from his analysis of society in his day. He considered that the dominant challenge to faith in the modern age lay in the secular approach to life promoted by the West. He felt that modern secularism had two faces. On the one hand, there was communism that explicitly denied God's existence and consciously fought against the place of religion in society. On the other, there was the secularism of modern capitalist systems which did not deny God's existence, but simply ignored the question of God and promoted a consumerist, materialist way of life as if there were no God or as though God had no moral will for humankind. In both types of secular society, some individuals might make a personal, private choice to follow a religious path, but religion should have nothing to say about politics, economics or the organization of society.

Said Nursi held that in the situation of this modern world, religious believers—Christian as well as Muslim—face a similar struggle, that is, the challenge to lead a life of faith in which the purpose of human life is to worship God and to love others in obedience to God's will, and to lead this life of faith in a world whose political, economic and social spheres are often dominated either by a militant atheism, such as that of communism, or by a practical atheism, where God is simply ignored, forgotten, or considered irrelevant.

Said Nursi insists that the threat posed by modern secularism to a living faith in God is real and that believers must truly struggle to defend the centrality of God's will in everyday life, but he does not advocate violence to pursue this goal. He says that the most important need today is for the greatest struggle, *al-jihad al-akbar* of which the Qur'an speaks. This is the interior effort to bring every aspect of one's life into submission to God's will. As he explained in his famous Damascus Sermon, one element of this greatest struggle is the necessity of acknowledging and overcoming one's own weaknesses and those of one's nation. Too often, he says, believers are tempted to blame their problems on others when the real fault lies in themselves—the dishonesty, corruption, hypocrisy and favoritism that characterize many so-called "religious" societies.

He further advocates the struggle of speech, *kalam*, what might be called a critical dialogue aimed at convincing others of the need to submit one's life to God's will. Where Said Nursi is far ahead of his time is that he foresees that in this struggle to carry on a critical dialogue with modern society Muslims should not act alone but must work together with those he calls "true Christians," in other words, Christians not in name only, but those who have interiorized the message which Christ brought, who practice their faith, and who are open and willing to cooperate with Muslims.

In contrast to the popular way in which many Muslims of his day looked at things, Said Nursi holds Muslims must not say that Christians are the enemy. Rather, Muslims and Christians have three common enemies that they have to face together: ignorance, poverty, dissension. In short, he sees the need for dialogue as arising from the challenges posed by secular society to Muslims and Christians and that dialogue should lead to a common stand favoring education, including ethical and spiritual formation to oppose the evil of ignorance, cooperation in development and welfare projects to oppose the evil of poverty, and efforts to unity and solidarity to oppose the enemy of dissension, factionalism, and polarization.

Said Nursi still hopes that before the end of time true Christianity will eventually be transformed into a form of Islam, but the differences that exist today between Islam and Christianity must not be considered obstacles to Muslim-Christian cooperation in facing the challenges of modern life. In fact, near the end of his life, in 1953, Said Nursi paid a visit in İstanbul to the Ecumenical Patriarch of the Orthodox Church to encourage Muslim-Christian dialogue. A few years earlier, in 1951, he sent a collection of his writings to Pope Pius XII, who acknowledged the gift with a handwritten note.

The particular talent of Said Nursi was his ability to interpret the Qur'anic teaching in such a way that it could be applied by modern Muslims to situations of modern life. His voluminous writings which have been gathered together into the *Risale-i Nur* the Message of Light express the need for a revitalization of society by the practice of everyday virtues like labor, mutual assistance, self-awareness, and moderation in possessions and deportment.

M. Fethullah Gülen: A Muslim Activist Who Practices Dialogue

How can the call to dialogue between believing Muslims and believing Christians be put into practice by the followers of Said Nursi? How can his directives to struggle together against the common enemies of ignorance, poverty and disunity be put into practice in a world which has continued to evolve in ways that are sometimes encouraging and in other ways that are quite disturbing? This is the challenge taken up by a contemporary Turkish activist, Muhammed Fethullah Gülen (1941–). Gülen never met Said Nursi and, while he speaks highly of Bediüzzaman and claims to have been greatly influenced by his writings, he denies being a "Nurcu" or follower of Said Nursi in any sectarian sense.

However, some scholars consider the movement associated with Gülen as one of the transformations that have occurred as Said Nursi's thought continues to be reinterpreted and applied anew in evolving historical and geographical situations. One scholar to study the movement Professor Hakan Yavuz, a Turkish scholar at the University of Utah, notes that "Some Turkish Nurcus, such as Yeni Asya of Mehmet Kutlular and the Fethullah Gülen community, reimagined the movement as a 'Turkish Islam'." Another scholar, Dr. İhsan Yılmaz concurs: "Nursi's discourse 'has already weathered major economic, political, and educational transformations'... Today, the Hizmet Movement is a manifestation of this phenomenon."

Where Gülen most clearly answers the call of Said Nursi is by taking up the challenge to combat ignorance. There are now over 300 schools around the world inspired by the convictions of Mr. Gülen, set up, administered, and staffed by his circle of students and associates. The schools try to bring together educational objectives that are too often dispersed among various school systems. They seek to give a strong scientific grounding, together with character formation in non-material values, which includes cultural, ethical, religious and spiritual training. In addition to the formal education carried out in schools, Fethullah Gülen's movement has pursued non-formal education through television and radio channels, newspapers and magazines, cultural and professional foundations.

Fethullah Gülen and his movement have also been active in the area of interreligious dialogue and peacemaking. Four years ago, Mr. Gülen traveled to Rome where he was met by Pope John Paul II. He has met the Ecumenical Patriarch of the Orthodox Church numerous times. His interreligious activities have gone beyond Muslim-Christian relations to include meetings with Jewish leaders at the national and international level. In connection with the Parliament of the World's Religions, held in cape Town, South Africa, Mr. Gülen delivered a major address on the theme: "The Necessity of Interfaith Dialogue: a Muslim Approach."

Mr. Gülen's was one of the first Muslim voices heard in condemnation of the terrorist acts committed on 11 September 2001. Within 24 hours of the tragedy, Mr. Gülen wrote an open letter in which he stated: "What lies behind certain Muslim people or institutions that misunderstand Islam getting involved in terrorist attacks that occur throughout the world should be sought not in Islam, but within those people themselves, in their misinterpretations, and in other factors. Just as Islam is not a religion of terrorism, any Muslim who correctly understands Islam cannot be thought of as a terrorist."[30]

As a Christian involved in working with Muslims and other religious believers for peace through interreligious dialogue, I am grateful for the insights of Said Nursi and for the leadership in this field provided by Fethullah Gülen.

---

[30] "True Muslims Cannot Be Terrorists," en.fgulen.com/about-fethullah-gulen/messages/1052-true-muslims-cannot-be-terrorists

Two Frontrunners for Peace:
John Paul II and Fethullah Gülen

We live in a strange world. So many people are in favor of peace, and yet many people around the world suffer because they live in situations of conflict and war. I was at an international conference not long ago, with many speakers from various countries, religions, and ideologies. It will not surprise you to learn that all the speakers affirmed the firm desire of their group for peace and offered quite convincing arguments to show that these were not just empty words. They noted that they and their colleagues not only wanted peace, but they were working actively to bring it about. Some cynical part of our makeup might ask, with so many committed and talented persons and organizations working for peace, why peace is so difficult to achieve, why does the lack of peace seem to be an ever-present part of the human experience.

Part of the problem is that even though many might be working for peace, it only takes a few to destroy that peace. I have lived for many years in parts of Southeast Asia where the vast majority of people, of all religions, ethnic groups, and walks of life, thirst for peace and come together to take common action to build peace. Generally speaking, there is peace. People live together well and cooperate at the daily level for the good of all. Nevertheless, it only takes a few individuals or small groups, driven by anger, resentment or jealousy, to try to destroy that peace. Moreover, modern technology has made it possible for a very limited number of individuals to destroy the very peace that is desired by the vast majority.

So our world is one which is repeatedly fractured by suspicion, conflict, and war. The causes are many and complex, and the paths to peace difficult to comprehend and to follow. There is a paradox here that we must face. It seems like everyone is in favor of peace, no one ever admits to being against peace, and yet there is very little peace in the world. The problem, I believe, lies in the fact that we are all in favor of peace *in the abstract*, but without saying in what peace consists, and without examining what is involved in building peace.

Of those religious thinkers of modern times who have attempted to study the concept of peace to explore what is involved in establishing and maintaining peace, I want to compare the thought of two persons who have made a remarkable contribution to the topic. One is a Christian, Pope John Paul II, leader of the Catholic Church, and the other a Muslim, Mr. Fethullah Gülen.

My paper aims at sharing some of the wisdom found in the writings of two living figures, one Christian and the other Muslim. Here I hope to bring together the thinking of these two scholars and religious teachers into a kind of dialogue on the theme: "the ethics of peace." I will do this by summarizing the position of the Pope as the basis or point of view from which I will then read and explain the views of Fethullah Gülen as found in his many writings.

Pope John Paul II: The Twin Pillars of Justice and Forgiveness

In his approach to peace, Pope John Paul II follows a statement he made repeatedly over the years: "Peace stands on two pillars: *justice* and *forgiveness*." I believe that there is much to be said for this view. It affirms that *both* of these elements, justice and forgiveness, are necessary to achieve a genuine peace. Focusing on one without the other cannot produce real peace, and peace efforts and negotiations that do not put these two elements at the center of the matters to be addressed will not succeed. One element without the other is not enough for a real peace.

The first element, *justice*, seeks to redress the wrong done, unfair treatment corrected, material property restored, false judgments rectified, whereas the second, *pardon*, seeks to repair the human relations damaged and destroyed in the conflict.

Looking at conflicts from the perspective of justice focuses one's attention on the *victims* of injustice, on their plight, on the effects of violence, strife and oppression on innocent people, on the concrete ways in which their lives have been shattered. People suffer, not because of the forces of nature or biology, but because of the way they have been treated by others. Injustice is not a mystery in that it is possible to trace its sources in the history of human choices. People could act in other ways to others, but they have chosen to act unjustly. In any conflict, there are many victims, in multiple ways, on all sides, but the level of loss and suffering is not the same for all. Some have experienced more bitter injustice than others. It is those who are greater victims of injustice, humanly and materially, who will be obstacles to peace until their injustices are redressed.

Every nation, every religious or ethnic group, can draw up a long list of grievances that they have against each other, of wrongs that their group has suffered at the hands of the others. This is the human burden of the experience of past misdeeds that people bring into their relations with others which complicate the way that groups relate to one another, that give rise to suspicions which can poison all efforts at cooperation and reconciliation and that can flare up into violence the slightest provocation.

I believe that the Pope's focus on the injustice experienced by victims of oppression and wrongdoing, rather than merely on the geopolitical and economic issues which are often at the forefront of negotiated settlements is realistic. The Pope's reasoning is like this. Any real peace, if it is to go beyond a simple "cease-fire" or temporary cessation of hostilities, has to get to the heart of the conflict and try to heal the breach in human relations which was ruptured. When peoples are at war, when individuals are estranged and alienated from one another, they are angry, suspicious, and resentful of one another. They see the other as an enemy to be overcome, defeated, the object of retaliation, rather than a fellow-human with whom one ought to be reconciled. Thus, no talk about peace can proceed effectively without addressing the issue of broken relationships and without taking positive steps to repair those relations.

If one group or individual is being oppressed or treated unjustly by another, one cannot hope for peace between the two until there is justice. The Pope sees justice in two ways: firstly, as a human quality which a person can acquire and develop with God's powerful assistance, and secondly as a "legal guarantee," that is, part of the functioning of the national and international rule of law. The aim of justice, both as a personal quality and as an element of the international system of relations among peoples, is to insure "full respect for rights and responsibilities" and to carry out a "just distribution of benefits and burdens."

Justice is thus a first, indispensable condition for peace. Unless one person treats another justly, that is, with respect for the other's rights and duties and by giving them their proper share of what is due to them, there will be no peace between them. The same holds true between social groups, ethnic groups, peoples and nations. Where there is aggression, oppression, occupation, transgression, there can be no peace. First, justice has to be established, then peace can be built.

However, for true peace, justice alone is not enough. Justice can never, by itself, make up for the suffering of people that often has gone on for many years and decades. One can take as an example the case of many groups of refugees around the world. Even in the rare scenario of the possibility for the refugees to return to their land, how can people be recompensed for the years of suffering? In the more frequent situations where a return to one's homeland is not a viable option, what financial consider-ations could make up in justice for lost decades lived out in the inhumane conditions to which refugees are subjected?

Even if armed conflict passes, how can people ever hope to live together in peace after all the bitterness and violence that has passed between them for so long? Focusing solely on justice will not bring back lost years, lost relatives, lost trust, lost hopes. Something more is needed, on all sides of the conflict.

This is where pardon, the second pillar of peace, comes into play. Whenever violent conflict occurs, the human relations are damaged and must undergo a slow, painful process of healing. Pardon can seem like a "soft" element in the peace-building pro-cess, something more suited to do-gooders, bleeding hearts, and idealistic religious types than to hard-headed politicians and nego-tiators. However, forgiveness and reconciliation are just as essen-tial as elements of peace as is the focus on justice, and in fact much more difficult to achieve. This is where many religious and secu-lar NGO programs are providing a critical component of the peace-building process. By bringing together those who have lost family and neighbors in shooting and bombing incidents with those from the other side who have similar histories of loss, by facilitating and favoring the sharing of experience of past suffer-ing and discovering common hopes for the future, by enabling people on both sides to see "the enemy" as individuals who are not very different from oneself, these organizations of reconcilia-tion are playing a key role in the long-term effort to build peace.

Forgiveness can seem like weakness to those involved in a conflict. It is, as the Pope states, "a personal choice, a decision to go against the natural instinct to pay back evil with evil." In doing so, it always involves an *apparent* short-term loss, but brings about the possibility of achieving a *real* long-term gain. "Violence," the Pope notes, works exactly the opposite: "opting for an apparent short-term gain, but involving a real and permanent loss." Thus, forgiveness may seem like weakness but, in the Pope's words, "it demands great spiritual strength and moral courage."

It should not be surprising to discover that both Christianity and Islam lay great importance on the notions of justice and forgiveness, if these are to be the indispensable pre-conditions of peace. In the Gospel, Jesus taught his disciples: "You have heard it said, 'Love your neighbor and hate your enemy,' but I say to you 'Love your enemies and pray for those who persecute you.'" In a similar vein, the Qur'an permits vengeance up to the limits of strict justice but no farther, and then always adds: "But it is better to forgive."

Just as those whose primary focus is the struggle for justice must always remember that justice alone can go only so far toward peace, but never all the way, so also peace-builders whose focus is on forgiveness must never forget that no real reconciliation is possible if the sometimes harsh demands of justice are not being honestly addressed and conscientiously requited. I believe that there is much wisdom in the teaching of Pope John Paul II that true peace rests on the twin pillars of justice and forgiveness.

Fethullah Gülen: Respecting Differences to Avoid Mutual Destruction

Events of the past few years have underscored the importance of dialogue among people of faith for the effective pursuit of peace. Interreligious dialogue is an alternative to the much-discussed "clash of civilizations." Those who do not subscribe to the theory that a civilizational clash is inevitable are proposing instead a *dialogue of civilizations*, an exchange of views aimed at mutual enrichment, a sharing of insights that can lead all to a deeper understanding of the nature of God and God's will for humankind on this planet.

One of the most persuasive and influential voices in the Muslim community that has called for dialogue as a step to peace is

Fethullah Gülen. The movement inspired and guided by Fethullah Gülen is offering Muslims a way to live out Islamic values amidst the complex demands of modern societies and to engage in ongoing dialogue and cooperation with people of other religions.

From its origins in Turkey, the movement has spread rapidly, through its schools in many countries, through its cultural and media activities, and through the social projects and dialogue encounters of Turks in diaspora in Europe, North America, and Australia, to the point that the influence of the Hizmet Movement is being felt in virtually all regions where Muslims live as majorities or minorities. Gülen's movement is a call to Muslims to a greater awareness that Islam teaches the need for dialogue and that Muslims are called to be agents and witnesses to God's universal mercy. In his support of his views, Gülen employs his broad knowledge of the Islamic tradition to bring together the Qur'anic Scripture, the *hadith* reports from Muhammad, and the insights of Muslims down through the ages. In this way, he makes a convincing argument that tolerance, love, and compassion are genuinely Islamic values that Muslims have a duty to bring to the modern world.

Through his movement, Gülen invites non-Muslims to move beyond prejudice, suspicion, and half-truths so that they might arrive at an understanding what Islam is really about. Someone whose knowledge of Islam is limited to the headlines of the daily newspapers is likely to believe that the religion teaches terrorism, suicide attacks, oppression of women, and hatred for those outside its community. However, the movement associated with the name of Fethullah Gülen seeks to live out an interpretation of Islamic teaching leads the believer to truly spiritual values like forgiveness, inner peace, social harmony, honesty, and trust in God. In expressing the Islamic values derived from his vast knowledge of the Islamic sources and tradition, Gülen not only calls Muslims to engage in dialogue and to work for peace, but he engages the non-Muslim in a discussion of commonly held ideals.

On 8 February 1998, Gülen traveled to the Vatican to visit Pope John Paul II. This was a courageous act for which Gülen was much criticized in his native Turkey. In an interview which he gave the following April after the visit, Gülen defended his daring act in terms of seeking world peace and affirmed that he was acting in line with the behavior of the prophet Muhammad, who accepted terms of peace that some of his companions felt were disadvantageous. In the interview, Gülen said:

> Our age is a time of addressing intellects and hearts, an undertaking that requires a peaceful atmosphere with mutual trust and respect... In the peaceful atmosphere engendered by this treaty [Hudaybiyya], the doors of hearts were opened to Islamic truths. We have no intention of conquering lands or peoples, but we are resolved to contribute to world peace and a peaceful order and harmony by which our old world will find a last happiness before its final destruction.[31]

Gülen is convinced that working for peace is demanded as the proper expression of an Islamic way of life. It is commanded by the Qur'an as the better way. It is the starting point of dialogue. It is the precondition for serving both society and humanity. As Gülen stated:

> If we start our efforts for dialogue with the belief that "peace is better" (Al-Nisa 4:128), then we must demonstrate that we are on the side of peace at home and abroad. Indeed, peace is of the utmost importance to Islam; fighting and war are only secondary occurrences which are bound to specific reasons and conditions. In that respect, we can say that if an environment of peace where all can live in peace and security cannot be achieved in this land, then it would be impossible for us to do any good service for society or for humanity.[32]

---

[31] Mehmet Kamış, "Medeniyetler Buluşması," *Aksiyon*, 14 February 1998
[32] Fethullah Gülen, *Toward a Global Civilization of Love and Tolerance*, 50–51.

It is interesting to compare Gülen's views on the role of forgiveness in peacemaking with the above-cited words of John Paul II. In 2002, the Pope stated that forgiveness implies a short-term loss aimed at a long-term gain, the repair of damaged human relations, whereas violence is an apparent short-term gain which entails a long-term loss. In a 1996 article, Gülen encouraged Muslims to dialogue and tolerance with very similar words, stating:

> I would like to stress the fact that Muslims will lose nothing by employing dialogue, love, and tolerance. Muslims continuously seek the approval of God. This is the greatest gain of all. In that respect, things that may appear as losses to some people are seen as gains by Muslims which certain other events may actually be detrimental even when they appear to be lucrative.[33]

He goes so far to say that "Peace, love, forgiveness, and tolerance are fundamental to Islam. Other things are accidental." Although according to specific circumstances, recourse to war might sometimes be justified, this "lesser jihad" of the sword is secondary to the essence of Islam, summed up in the terms "peace, love, forgiveness, tolerance." Gülen accuses those who advocate war and violence of having been misled by a grossly literalist reading of the Qur'an. As a consequence, they misunderstand the nature of Islam. He states:

> It is necessary to give priority to basic Muslim issues according to their degree of importance. ... Unfortunately, those who ignore the essence and do so without taking into consideration the reasons for secondary rules and regulations, those who (by reading the Qur'an in the manner of a crude kind of superficial literalism) emphasize violence—these people have not understood the rules, the reasons for them, nor their source, nor have they understood Islam.[34]

---

[33] Ibid., 52.
[34] Fethullah Gülen, *Toward a Global Civilization of Love and Tolerance*, 71–72.

Ultimately, for Gülen, peace comes down to respecting the legitimate differences among peoples. Anything less means self-destruction. Gülen states:

> The peace of this (global) village lies in respecting all these differences, considering these differences to be part of our nature and in ensuring that people appreciate these differences. Otherwise, it is unavoidable that the world will devour itself in a web of conflicts, disputes, fights, and the bloodiest of wars, thus preparing the way for its own end.[35]

We all have much to gain from the insights on peace offered by these two frontrunners. Their teachings go hand-in-hand and complement one another. In their thinking, we find evidence that Christians and Muslims have much to learn from one another and that, when their respective faiths are deeply reflected upon, can lead to truly surprising coincidences of thought.

---

[35] Ibid., 250.

Love and Truth in Democratic Societies: Fethullah Gülen and Pope Benedict XVI on Social Questions

On June 29, 2009, Pope Benedict XVI issued a new encyclical letter entitled *Caritas in Veritate*, that is, *Love in Truth* or "Truth-filled Love." This letter was directed to Christians and to all those who are interested in facing seriously questions regarding democracy, justice, and development in our modern world. The influential Muslim scholar Fethullah Gülen, whose thought we are studying in this Congress, has also written extensively on many of these topics. In keeping with the Congress theme of "East and West Encounters," I will try to bring together the views of these two religious leaders in a type of "dialogue of ideas."

In presenting the views of Fethullah Gülen and Pope Benedict XVI on some of the social questions of our time, I do not intend to take a "comparative" approach of simply juxtaposing the ideas of one to those of the other, e.g., "Hocaefendi says this about democracy, and the Pope says that." Each of these men approaches the issues in his own way, and I propose to let each treat his central concerns as he sees fit. I hope that the flow will reflect that of a scholarly conversation between two intelligent and deeply religious believers, each of whom has exhaustive knowledge of his respective religious heritage and who has given much thought and prayer to the basic human issues that confront us all.

Religion and Democracy

Gülen. In what way can we speak about a particular religion and its relation to democracy? The question is pertinent because many newspaper articles and even scholarly papers purport to examine, for example, "Islam and democracy." One reason for the frequency of this approach is that many scholars are willing to treat religion solely as a sociological, economic, or political phenomenon, while denying or ignoring the spiritual, immutable, and trans-rational nature of religious faith. Gülen admits that even some Muslims raise issues about whether Islam and democracy are compatible and asks whether this kind of question is valid or can be productive of truth.

He holds that religion in general and Islam in particular cannot be compared on the same basis with democracy or any other political, social, or economic system. Political, social and economic systems are by their nature transient and variable. American democracy is not the same as German, Turkish, or French democracy, nor is American democracy today the same phenomenon that it was 40-50 years ago. By its very nature, every political system is subject to limitations of time and space. By contrast, religion deals with eternal, unchanging realities. Religious faith concerns the nature of God, the teaching of the prophets, the message of Scriptures, the existence of angels, and the expectation of Judgment; these are all matters which have nothing to do with changing times and temporary institutions.[36] Religion is concerned with the worship of God and the universal and unchanging standards of morality, which do not depend on changing times and worldly life. Thus, any comparison between religion and democracy or any other political system is bound to limp.

---

[36] Fethullah Gülen, "A Comparative Approach to Islam and Democracy," *Toward a Global Civilization of Love and Tolerance*, Somerset: The Light, 2006, p. 345. (2011 edition, p. 219.)

Benedict. In his encyclical, Benedict agrees that it is not the role of religion to propose technical solutions to political or economic problems, nor should religious communities be interfering in the politics of national states. The mission of the Church is, rather to speak the truth about individuals and societies, about human dignity and the human vocation. These are principles that are applicable in every political and economic system and remain equally valid at different periods of history. Without this concern for and focus on the truth, according to Pope Benedict, "it would be easy to fall into an empiricist and skeptical view of life, incapable of rising to the level of praxis because of a lack of interest in grasping the values—sometimes even the meanings—with which to judge and direct it."[37]

The point of correspondence between Gülen's thought and that of the Pope lies in the perennial nature of religion in confronting the ever-changing nature of political and economic life. For Benedict, the Church does not engage in problem-solving of technical matters that by their nature are bound up with situations unique to each time and place. Similarly, it is not the task of the Church to interfere in the politics of nations by which the constantly changing daily affairs of citizens are governed. The role of religion is, rather to ask and raise questions about truth that transcends particular events, systems, and individuals. If people of faith do not continually raise these ageless concerns of truth, we would all be condemned to be governed by spreadsheets, short-term forecasts, public opinion polls, and similar political and economic indicators.

For Gülen, matters of faith transcend the vicissitudes of history and the variations in political systems. Like Benedict, he sees religion as being concerned with the eternal truths of life and existence, what he calls "immutable principles related to faith, worship, and morality." Gülen confesses that Islam has worldly

---

[37] Benedict XVI, *Love in Truth* (*Caritas in Veritate*), par. 9.

aspects, although these come to no more than 5% of the teaching of the prophets. However, these aspects, despite their relative unimportance compared to eternal truths of faith, can be treated in the context of democracy.

The Varieties of Democratic Experience

As noted above, Gülen holds that democracy is not one thing, but is continually developing and constantly producing new variations. It is a system subject to continual development and constant revision. History's first well documented democracy, that of Athens, was what today would be called *direct* democracy, that is, direct rule by a free assembly of the people, but at the same time it was a *limited* democracy, in that women and slaves could not participate in it. Most of our modern states have not adopted the principle of direct democracy, but have opted, rather, for representative democracy, where sovereignty is exercised by elected officials. In a further variation, some countries, like many states of the United States, have what can be called *deliberative* democracy, which through the mechanisms of initiative, referendum, and recall introduce elements of direct democracy into a basically representative system.

Each country in the world has combined and adapted these basic democratic functions in its own way. Moreover, in every nation, its democratic processes are constantly being subjected to revision and fine-tuning. As elements of the process are found to be functioning poorly or immobilized by constitutional crisis, new refinements are introduced to which the populace gives but a provisional commitment. Otherwise, the system is pragmatically allowed to stand for the time being, always with the awareness that the actual form any democracy takes at any given time is tentative and impermanent.

Gülen. Gülen's view that democracy is a system that is continually being developed and revised is thus a point well taken.

One cannot make universal, sweeping statements about democracy and its compatibility with religion without taking into account the tentative and passing nature of all democracies, as well as the variations that occur according to region, culture, and circumstance. Therefore, it is not the role of Islam or any other religion to propose or endorse any unchangeable form of government or to attempt to shape its institutions.[38] What the religion of Islam does is to establish fundamental principles that should orient the general character and standards of a government, while leaving people free to choose the type and form of government most suitable according to the demands of time and circumstances.[39] Thus, it is natural and proper for Muslim organizations and movements, just like other members of civil society, to propose principles and values for the consideration of government authorities.

Benedict. We can note the correspondence of these views with those of Benedict XVI in his recent encyclical: "The State does not need to have identical characteristics everywhere. The support aimed at strengthening weak constitutional systems can easily be accompanied by the development of other political players, of a cultural, social, territorial or religious nature, alongside the State. The articulation of political authority at the local, national and international levels is one of the best ways of giving direction to the process of economic globalization. It is also the way to ensure that it does not actually undermine the foundations of democracy."[40]

The Pope is suggesting that political flexibility is needed today in order for governments to control and regulate the complex interactions and often-instantaneous transactions of globalized economics. The improved capabilities of democracies to deal with economic globalization depends both upon the increased effec-

---

[38] Fethullah Gülen, *Toward a Global Civilization of Love and Tolerance*, 346.

[39] Fethullah Gülen, "A Comparative Approach to Islam and Democracy," 134.

[40] Benedict XVI, *Love in Truth (Caritas in Veritate)*, par. 41.

tiveness of local, national and international authority as well as on the simultaneous strengthening of other sectors of civil society, religious as well as cultural and regional.

Characteristics of Democratic Societies

Gülen. According to Gülen, in democratic societies, people govern themselves as opposed to being ruled by someone above. Hence, in a democracy, it is the individual that has priority over the community. On the one hand, the just rights and aspirations of the individual must not be stifled by communitarian expediency while, on the other, individualism is not an absolute value in itself. In order to live in society, individuals must adjust to realities and limit their own freedoms. This ongoing process of adjustment, balancing the claims of the individual with the demands of the community, is one that is occurring with greater or lesser success in every country today.

In applying these standards to his native Turkey, Gülen is optimistic, but he does not shy away from self-criticism. "Democratization is an irreversible process in Turkey," he states in response to those who claim that his movement seeks to overthrow the Turkish Republic.[41] Nevertheless, the democratic ideal still lags behind that of other countries: "Standards of democracy and justice [in Turkey] must be elevated to the level of our contemporaries in the West," he said in an interview with the *Turkish Daily News.*[42]

Benedict. For Pope Benedict, the great advantage of democracy, and the reason why he urges Christians to support faithfully this political option, is that of all systems of government,

---

[41] Fethullah Gülen, "Interview" in *Sabah*, 27 January 1995, cited in M. Hakan Yavuz "The Gülen Movement: the Turkish Puritans," 28.

[42] Fethullah Gülen, "Turkey Assails a Revered Islamic Moderate."

"democracy alone can guarantee equality and rights to everyone."[43] It is the conviction that democracy is that form of government that can best guarantee justice for the most people that recommends it to the Pope. "There is a reciprocal dependence between democracy and justice," he holds, "that impels everyone to work responsibly to safeguard each person's rights, especially those of the weak and marginalized."

It could even be said that the achievement of justice and a dignified life for all, especially the most vulnerable, is one of the main goals of democracy. Benedict holds that "Democracy will attain its full actualization only when every person and each people have access to the primary goods (life, food, water, health care, education, work and the certainty of their rights) through an ordering of internal and international relations that assures each person of the possibility of participating in them."[44]

Gülen. Gülen arrives at a similar position by applying principles drawn from the Islamic ethical tradition. Starting from the standard of equality enunciated in a *hadith* from the Prophet Muhammad, Gülen holds that no individual, family, or ethnic group has any inherent "right to rule," nor does wealth or power bestow any political privileges. The political ethics taught by Islam can be summed up in six principles:

    a. Power derives from truth, not truth from power.

    b. Indispensability of justice and rule of law.

    c. Individual rights: life, belief, property, reproduction, health.

    d. Privacy and immunity of the individual.

    e. No conviction without evidence, no punishment for another's crimes.

---

[43] Benedict XVI, "Address to the Italian Christian Workers' Associations (A.C.L.I.)."

[44] Benedict XVI, "Address to Members of the 'Centesimus Annus' Foundation."

    f.   Administration through consultation.[45]

So long as these principles are followed, Islamic teaching can accept a variety of governmental systems. Muhammed Çetin notes that "According to Gülen the understanding of democracy and human rights within the theoretical heritage of Islam is not dogmatic but it centers around values such as compromise, stability, the protection of the life, honor and dignity of the human being, justice, equity, dialogue, and consultation."[46] Greg Barton agrees: "Gülen frequently endorses democracy specifically, arguing that it is the most appropriate form of government for the modern period and one that is entirely compatible with Islam."[47] Similarly, while Islamic faith can be lived out in a variety of social and political contexts, the Islamic values that should embody this way of life are those taught in the Qur'an. In this regard, Gülen mentions the primacy of truth or right over force, and the ideals of love, mutual respect, assistance, and social education.[48]

Benedict. For Benedict XVI, the reciprocal link between democracy and justice is oriented toward achieving integral human development so that all people can live in a way compatible with their human dignity. By "integral human development" he understands "the goal of rescuing peoples, first and foremost, from hunger, deprivation, endemic diseases and illiteracy. From the economic point of view, this means their active participation, on equal terms, in the international economic process; from the social point of view, it means their evolution into educated societies marked by solidarity; from the political point of view, it

---

45 Fethullah Gülen, *Toward a Global Civilization of Love and Tolerance*, 347.

46 Muhammed Çetin, "Fethullah Gülen and the Contribution of Islamic Scholarship to Democracy, *The Fountain* 67: January – February, 2009.

47 Greg Barton, "Preaching by Example and Learning for Life: Understanding the Gülen *Hizmet* in the Global Context of Religious Philanthropy and Civil Religion," 655.

48 Fethullah Gülen, *Toward a Global Civilization of Love and Tolerance*, 351.

means the consolidation of democratic regimes capable of ensuring freedom and peace."[49]

Where the demands of justice are not met, the very functioning of democracy is in danger. The Pope envisions justice as permitting trust, on which all social solidarity depends. He explains: "Through the systemic increase of social inequality, both within a single country and between the populations of different countries (i.e. the massive increase in relative poverty), not only does social cohesion suffer, thereby placing democracy at risk, but so too does the economy, through the progressive erosion of 'social capital'—the network of relationships of trust, dependability, and respect for rules, all of which are indispensable for any form of civil coexistence."[50]

Although they differ in phrasing, there is much in common between Gülen's Islamic vision and the Christian ideal expressed by the Pope. For both, true democracy, which is based on justice and oriented toward the common good of human development, is informed by the values expressed in religious insight. For Gülen, it is the Islamic virtues of truth, love, solidarity, assistance and mutual respect. For Benedict, it is truth, love, participation, solidarity, and peace.

Religious Freedom

Gülen. According to Gülen, the type of government recommended by Islamic teaching is one based on a social contract between the governors and the governed. The ideal envisioned by the Islamic tradition is that of a representative system in which the legislators and executives are elected by the people, who establish a *majlis* or parliament, debate issues, and pass laws in accord with the will of the people. In this way, the society as a whole participates in auditing and holding responsible the administra-

---

[49] Benedict XVI, *Love in Truth* (*Caritas in Veritate*), par. 21.
[50] Benedict XVI, *Love in Truth*, par. 32.

tion.[51] Although these are the principles that characterize virtually all the modern democracies, Gülen explains that these principles of governance accepted by modern people around the world
today are the same as those taught by Islam. Gülen is careful to
spell out this compatibility in response to the chorus of critics
who continue to ask whether the religion of Islam is compatible
with democracy.

For this reason, Gülen emphasizes that these are not simply
his own ideas but are, rather, the social values taught by the
Islamic tradition itself. He notes that in the time of the first four
caliphs, the principles of democracy and free elections were followed. Even when, after the death of Ali, governance of the
Islamic *umma* was transformed from caliphate into a hereditary
sultanate, many of the features of modern democracies were still
being practiced. He points out, for example, that Jews and Christians enjoyed religious rights under the rule of Islamic governments and that respect for minority rights consistently forms part
of the heritage of Islamic values.

Benedict. The importance of religious freedom is one that
Gülen shares with Benedict XVI, who emphasized the point when
he spoke to the representatives of other religions who gathered
to meet him on his trip to Washington, D.C., in April 2008. He
pointed out that, in order to protect the rights to religious freedom, particularly of minorities, it is not sufficient to pass laws to
prohibit discrimination. Compliance requires vigilance and
monitoring on the part of all. He went on: "The task of upholding
religious freedom is never completed. New situations and challenges invite citizens and leaders to reflect on how their decisions
respect this basic human right. Protecting religious freedom
within the rule of law does not guarantee that peoples—particularly minorities—will be spared unjust forms of discrimination
and prejudice. This requires constant effort on the part of all
members of society to ensure that citizens are afforded the oppor-

---

51   Gülen, *Toward a Global Civilization of Love and Tolerance*, 350.

tunity to worship peaceably and to pass on their religious heritage to their children."[52]

Similarly, one might say, it is not sufficient for each religious group to defend the rights of its own members, e.g., Christians defending the rights of Christians, Muslims those of Muslims etc. Rather, everyone has an obligation to defend the rights to religious freedom of whatever group is suffering from discrimination or injustice. Moreover, the witness of each religion to the importance of religious freedom as a basic human right will be more credible and powerful if the followers of various religions would world together to defend this right. It is especially incumbent on members of the majority group, which usually have greater access to political and social authorities, to support the just causes of religious minorities, and their willingness to sustain minority rights is a measure of their own credibility.

Democracy and Holistic Development

Gülen. If there is one area in which the thought of Gülen and Benedict XVI most strongly coincide it is the conviction that social systems must address the whole person. According to Gülen, any attempt at treating people solely as *homo economicus* or *homo politicus*, disregarding the spiritual dimension of the human person and the spiritual needs that flow from the immaterial aspects of human nature, is doomed to failure. Gülen is convinced, rather, that if democracy takes a holistic approach to the human person, it can be the instrument for permitting greater opportunities for happiness to the greatest number of people. He makes this eloquent appeal: "If human beings are considered as a whole, without disregarding the spiritual dimension of their existence and their spiritual needs, and without forgetting that human life is not limited to this mortal life and that all people have a great

52 Benedict XVI, "Address to the Representatives of Other Religions."

craving for eternity, democracy could reach the peak of perfection and bring even more happiness to humanity."[53]

Benedict. In the final section of his encyclical *Caritas in veritate*, Benedict XVI arrives at a similar position. He affirms that "Development must include not just material growth but also spiritual growth," since the human person is a "unity of body and soul," born of God's creative love and destined for eternal life.[54] When a someone is far from God, that person becomes unsettled, ill at ease, and social and psychological alienation set in. He holds that "the many neuroses that afflict affluent societies are attributable in part to spiritual factors," and new types of slavery in the form of hopelessness and addictions can be explained by economic development and political freedom without corresponding attention to spiritual growth. He concludes: "There cannot be holistic development and universal common good unless people's spiritual and moral welfare is taken into account, considered in their totality as body and soul."[55]

Conclusion: The Contribution of Islamic Humanism and Christian Humanism to Democracy and Development

Because of the essential component of the spiritual to the integral growth of the human person in society, religions such as Islam and Christianity have an indispensable contribution to make to the growth of democracy and human development, just as they have an inescapable responsibility to offer their societies the insights arising from their spiritual experience. As Gülen puts it: "I believe that Islam also would enrich democracy in answering the deep needs of humans, such as spiritual satisfaction, which

---

53 Gülen, *Toward a Global Civilization of Love and Tolerance*, 352.
54 Benedict XVI, *Love in Truth*, par. 76.
55 Ibid.

cannot be fulfilled except through the remembrance of the Eternal One."[56]

If Gülen is calling for "an Islamic humanism" on the part of Muslims, Benedict's conviction that what is needed for genuine development is a "Christian humanism" on the part of Christians. He says:

> The greatest service to development is a Christian humanism that enkindles love and takes its lead from truth, accepting both as a lasting gift from God. Ideological rejection of God and an atheism of indifference, oblivious to the Creator and at risk of becoming equally oblivious to human values, constitute some of the chief obstacles to development today. A humanism that excludes God is an inhuman humanism. Only humanism open to the Absolute can guide us in the promotion and building of forms of social and civic life—structures, institutions, culture and ethos—without exposing us to the risk of becoming ensnared by the fashions of the moment.[57]

Almost 100 years ago, the Muslim scholar Said Nursi called on his students to unite with genuine Christians in opposing atheistic and materialistic tendencies that, according to the teachings of all the prophets, must inevitably result in destructive and self-destructive human behavior. Nursi felt that true Muslims and Christians had a common mission to save modern societies from heedless tendencies that cause human misery. I believe that in our day, these two thinkers—Fethullah Gülen and Pope Benedict XVI, one Muslim and the other Christian—can give us a sound conceptual basis on which we can discuss, in truth and love, the contribution that by our obedience to God we can offer together to our modern societies.

---

[56] Fethullah Gülen, "An Interview with Fethullah Gülen," 452.
[57] Benedict XVI, *Love in Truth*, par. 78.

Gülen as Educator

The So-called Gülen Schools

T he topic that I chose for this paper is that of Fethullah
Gülen as an educator. I must confess at the outset that I
have arrived at the topic of my talk backwards. Rather
than having studied the writings of Fethullah Gülen on education
and pedagogy and then tried to see, in what might be called a
deductive approach, how he has put these principles into practice, I have instead come to know first the educational institutions conducted by participants of the movement led by Mr.
Gülen. This has led me in turn to study his writings to discover
the rationale that lies behind the tremendous educational venture that has ensued from the educational vision of Fethullah
Gülen and his colleagues.

At the outset, it is necessary to be precise about the relationship of Mr. Gülen to the schools that are often loosely called "Gülen
schools," or "schools of the Hizmet Movement." Mr. Gülen describes
himself primarily as an educator and is generally referred to by
members of his movement as Hocaefendi, a title of respect given
to religious teachers in Turkey.[58] However, he is careful to dis-

---

[58] Gülen has had to defend his movement from accusations that the title
      Hocaefendi indicates a kind of sect, quasi-Sufi *tariqah*, or Ottoman reviv-
      alist usage. The term, he says, has no hierarchical significance or official
      connotation, but is simply "a respectful way of addressing someone whose
      knowledge on religious matters is recognized and acknowledged by the
      general public." Cited in Lynne Emily Webb, *Fethullah Gülen: Is There
      More to Him than Meets the Eye*, 80.

tinguish between education and teaching. "Most human beings can be teachers," he states, "but the number of educators is severely limited."[59]

He has also tried to make clear that he has no schools of his own. "I'm tired of saying that I don't have any schools,"[60] he affirms with a bit of exasperation. The more than 1000 elementary schools, high schools, college preparatory institutions, dormitories, and universities in over 140 countries that are associated with his name stem from a circle of students, colleagues and businessmen who formed about Fethullah Gülen in the 1960s.[61] The schools have been established by individual agreements between the countries in which they are located and the educational companies founded for this purpose. Each school is an independently run institution, but most of the schools rely on the services of Turkish companies to provide educational supplies and human resources. After completing his studies in the *madrasa* in Erzurum, he began teaching in Edirne in 1958. Shortly thereafter, he transferred to İzmir, where a small group of like-minded educators and students became the nucleus of the movement. It is from this circle of educators, whose number has grown dramatically over the years, that the schools associated with the name of Fethullah Gülen have been founded. Operating independently, but maintaining links of coordination and training, the schools could be called a loose federation of institutions that share a common pedagogic vision, similar curriculum, and human and material resources.

[59] Fethullah Gülen, *Criteria or Lights of the Way*, I, 36.
[60] Cited in Webb, *Fethullah Gülen: Is There More to Him than Meets the Eye*, 106.
[61] Citing *The Economist*, Yılmaz estimates the number of followers and sympathizers of Gülen's movement at somewhere between 200,000 and 4,000,000. İhsan Yılmaz, "Changing Turkish-Muslim Discourses on Modernity, West and Dialogue," footnote 33.

My Personal Encounter with "Gülen Schools"

My first encounter with one of these schools dates back to 1995, in Zamboanga, on the southern Philippine island of Mindanao, when I learned that there was a "Turkish" school several miles outside the city. On approaching the school, the first thing that caught my attention was the large sign at the entrance to the property bearing the name: "The Philippine-Turkish School of Tolerance." This is a startling affirmation in Zamboanga, a city almost equally 50% Christian and 50% Muslim, located in a region where for over 20 years various Moro separatist movements have been locked in an armed struggle against the military forces of the government of the Philippines.

I was well-received by the Turkish director and staff of the school, where over 1000 students study and live in dormitories. As I learned from the Turkish staff and their Filipino colleagues, both Muslim and Christian, the affirmation of their school as an institution dedicated towards formation in tolerance was no empty boast. In a region where kidnapping is a frequent occurrence, along with guerrilla warfare, summary raids, arrests, disappearances, and killings by military and para-military forces, the school is offering Muslim and Christian Filipino children, along with an educational standard of high quality, a more positive way of living and relating to each other. My Jesuit colleagues and the lay professors at the Ateneo de Zamboanga confirm that from its beginning, the Philippine-Turkish School of Tolerance has maintained a deep level of contact and cooperation with Christian institutions of the region.

Since that time I have had occasion to visit other schools in the Fethullah Gülen network and discuss educational policy with the teaching and administrative staff. In Turkey, I have visited several institutions in the İstanbul area and in the city of Urfa. In Kyrgyzstan, a former Soviet republic in Central Asia, I had the opportunity to examine at length about half the twelve Sebat schools, including the new Atatürk Alatoo University, all inspired and founded by the Hizmet Movement. I can state without quali-fication that I find these schools to be one of the most dynamic and worthwhile educational enterprises that I have encountered in the world today.

The strength of their programs in the sciences, informatics, and languages is shown in their repeated successes in academic olympiads. In a junior high school in Bishkek, I addressed a group of seventh-grade Kyrgyz children for about a half-hour. At the end of my talk, the teacher asked the students to identify those elements of pronunciation and vocabulary that showed that I was speaking an American rather than a British form of English, and to my amazement the children had no difficulty in doing so. Although English was the language of instruction in this school, as is usual in the Gülen schools outside Turkey, the students seemed equally competent in Russian and Turkish, in addition to their native Kyrgyz. The dedication and *esprit d'corps* of the teachers give evidence that they are conscious of being engaged in an exciting educational venture. Nowhere did I encounter any signs of the malaise and apparent confusion that so often afflicts schools in developing countries.

Aware that these schools are a manifestation of a religious commitment of Muslims, I had expected to find a more explicitly Islamic content to the curriculum and the physical environment, but this was not the case. When I asked about the surprising absence of what to me would have been an understandable part of a religiously-inspired educational project, I was told that because of the pluralist nature of the student bodies—Christian and Mus-lim in Zamboanga, and Buddhist and Hindu as well in Kyrgyz-stan—that what they sought to communicate were universal Islamic values such as honesty, hard work, harmony, and consci-entious service rather than any confessional instruction. In the Sebat International School in Bishkek, students from U.S.A., Korea, and Turkey appeared to be studying comfortably with those com-ing from Afghanistan and Iran.

These encounters led me to study the writings of Fethullah Gülen to ascertain the educational principles and motivation which undergird the schools and to try to find Gülen's own techniques that have made him into an educator capable of inspiring others with his vision. These are the questions that will occupy the remainder of my paper. I will concentrate mainly on the Gülen schools as the central expression of his educational policies, and must pass over in silence the educational aspects of other ventures which he has promoted, such as the Samanyolu television network, the *Zaman* newspaper and other publishing projects, the scholarship program for needy students, and the efforts of the Writers and Journalists Foundation to promote interreligious dialogue and understanding.

Gülen's Educational Vision

Gülen's educational starting point would seem to be what he sees as a fundamental crisis in Turkish society. Analyzing the factors that have contributed to bring about this societal crisis, he concludes that an element which cannot be dismissed is the lack of coordination[62] among the various types and systems of education. He regards the development of education in Turkey throughout the 20th Century as an unhealthy competition among mutually exclusive systems of education, which has produced graduates who lack an integrated perspective towards the future and perpetuate the existing divisions in society. He states: "At a time when modern schools concentrated on ideological dogmas, institutions of religious education (*madrasas*) broke with life, institutions of spiritual training (*takyas*) were immersed in sheer metaphysics, and the army restricted itself to sheer force, this coordination was essentially not possible."[63]

---

[62] I believe that the term "integration" conveys Mr. Gülen's intent better in English than "coordination."

[63] Fethullah Gülen, *Towards the Lost Paradise*, 11.

Modern secular schools, he holds, have been unable to free themselves of the prejudices and conventions of modernist ideology, while the *madrasas* have shown little interest or capability to meet the challenges of technology and scientific thought. The *madrasas* lack the flexibility, vision, and ability to break with past, enact change, and offer the type of educational formation that is needed today. The Sufi-oriented *takyas*, which traditionally had fostered the development of spiritual values, have lost their dynamism and, as Gülen puts it, "console themselves with virtues and wonders of the saints who had lived in previous centuries."[64] The educational training offered by the military, which had in previous times been the representative of religious energy and activity and a symbol of national identity, has devolved into an espousal of attitudes of self-assertion and self-preservation.

The challenge today is to find a way in which these traditional pedagogical systems can move beyond regarding each other as rivals or enemies so that they can learn from one another. By integrating the insights and strengths found in the various educational currents, educators must seek to bring about a "marriage of mind and heart" if they hope to form individuals of "thought, action, and inspiration."[65] An integration of the interior wisdom which is the cumulative heritage built up over the centuries with the scientific tools essential for the continued progress of the nation would enable students to move beyond the societal pressures of their environment and provide them with both internal stability and direction for their actions. He states: "Until we help them through education, the young will be captives of their environment. They wander aimlessly, intensely moved by their passions, but far from knowledge and reason. They can become truly valiant young representatives of national

---

[64] Ibid.
[65] Ibid., 12.

thought and feeling, provided their education integrates them with their past, and prepares them intelligently for the future."[66]

This last phrase is important and would appear to be Gülen's answer to an ongoing debate in Turkey. *"Integrate them with their past, and prepare them intelligently for the future."* Many observers have noted that one of the characteristic features of the modern Republic of Turkey has been its concerted effort to *break* with the Ottoman past. Many of the laws enacted in the past 70 years by the Turkish government have consciously sought to break with the Ottoman past as a way of modernizing the nation. Examples could be given in the change of capital from İstanbul to Ankara, the abolition of the caliphate/sultanate, the orthographic reform of replacing Arabic script by Roman letters and the language reform of substituting Arabic and Persian terms with words of Turkish roots, the legal reform in which the Swiss civil code and Italian penal code were adopted in place of *sharia* regulations, the establishment of Sunday as the weekly day of rest, the enforced use of surnames and the replacement of the Persian -*zadeh* by the Turkish -*oğlu* suffix, the prescription of Western dress along with the prohibition of characteristic Ottoman clothing such as fez and turban. All these reforms were aimed at breaking with the Ottoman past in an effort to modernize.[67]

In the decades since the establishment of the Turkish Republic, many Turkish Muslims have criticized the "modernization" program undertaken by the government for blindly adopting the best and worst of European civilization. They have seen secularization as not merely an unintended by-product of the secularization process, but rather as the conscious result of an anti-religious bias. They contend that the unspoken presumption that underlay the modernizing reforms has been an ideological conviction that religion is an obstacle to progress and must be exclud-

---

[66] Gülen, *Criteria or Lights of the Way*, I, 59.
[67] Bernard Lewis, *The Emergence of Modern Turkey*, 268-289.

ed from the public sphere of society, economics, and politics if the nation is to move forward. The battle lines drawn up during the decades since the establishment of the Republic, and reinforced by the mutually competitive systems of education, have made the religion-secularization debate in Turkey one in which every thinker is expected to declare their allegiance.

One of the reasons why, in my opinion, Fethullah Gülen has been often attacked by both "right" and "left," by "secular" and "religious" in Turkey is precisely because he has refused to take sides on an issue which he regards as a dead-end. He is instead offering a future-oriented approach by which he hopes to move beyond the ongoing debate. Gülen's solution is to affirm the intended goal of modernization enacted by the Turkish Republic, but to show that a truly effective process of modernization must include the development of the whole person. In educational terms, it must take the major concerns of the various existing streams of education and weave them into a new educational style which will respond to changing demands of today's world.

This is very different from reactionary projects which seek to revive or restore the past. Denying that the education offered in the schools associated with his name is an attempt to restore the Ottoman system or to reinstate the caliphate, Gülen repeatedly affirms that the schools are oriented towards the future. He cites an ancient Turkish adage, "If there is no adaptation to new conditions, the result will be extinction."[68]

Despite the necessity of modernization, he holds, there are nevertheless risks involved in any radical break with the past. Cut off from traditional values, young people are in danger of being educated with no values at all beyond those of material success. Non-material values such as profundity of ideas, clarity of thought, depth of feeling, cultural appreciation, or interest in

---

[68]   Webb, 86.

spirituality tend to be ignored in modern educational ventures which are largely aimed at mass-producing functionaries of a globalized market system.[69]

Such students might be adequately prepared to find jobs, but they will not have the necessary interior formation to achieve true human freedom. Leaders in both economic and political fields often favor and promote job-oriented, "value-free" education because it enables those with power to control the "trained but not educated" working cadres more easily. "Gülen asserts that if you wish to keep masses under control, simply starve them in the area of knowledge. They can escape such tyranny only through education. The road to social justice is paved with adequate, universal education, for only this will give people sufficient understanding and tolerance to respect the rights of others."[70] Thus, in Gülen's view, it is not only the establishment of justice which is hindered by the lack of well-rounded education, but also the recognition of human rights and attitudes of acceptance and tolerance toward others. If people are properly educated to think for themselves and to espouse the positive values of social justice, human rights and tolerance, they will be able to be agents of change to implement these beneficial goals.

The crisis in modern societies arises from decades of schooling having produced "generations with no ideals."[71] It is human ideals, aims, goals, and vision which are the source of movement, action, and creativity in society. People whose education has been limited to the acquisition of marketable skills are no longer able to produce the dynamism needed to inspire and carry out societal change. The result is social atrophy, decadence, and narcissism. He states: "When [people] are left with no ideals or aims,

---

[69] Gülen, *Towards the Lost Paradise*, 16.

[70] "M. Fethullah Gülen: A Voice of Compassion, Love, Understanding and Dialogue," Introduction to M. Fethullah Gülen, "The Necessity of Interfaith Dialogue: a Muslim Approach," 4.

[71] Gülen, *Towards the Lost Paradise*, 51-52.

they become reduced to the condition of animated corpses, showing no signs of distinctively human life.... Just as an inactive organ becomes atrophied, and a tool which is not in use becomes rusty, so aimless generations will eventually waste away because they lack ideals and aims."[72]

The societal crisis is intensified by the fact that, in his judgment, the teachers and intelligentsia, who should be the guides and movers of society, have allowed themselves to become perpetuators of a restrictive and non-integrated approach to education. Rather than raising their voices in protest against the elimination of humane values from the educational system and campaigning for a pedagogy that integrates scientific preparation with non-material values studied in the disciplines of logic, ethics, culture, and spirituality, the educators themselves too often "readily adapted to the new low standard."[73] He finds it difficult to understand how intellectuals could prefer the spiritually impoverished and technologically obsessed modern culture to a traditional cultural foundation that had grown in sophistication and subtlety over the centuries.

It follows that if educational reform is to be accomplished, teacher training is a task that cannot be ignored. Gülen notes that "education is different from teaching. Most human beings can be teachers, but the number of educators is severely limited."[74] The difference between the two lies in that both teachers and educators impart information and teach skills, but the educator is one who has the ability to assist the students' personalities to emerge, who fosters thought and reflection, who builds character and enables the student to interiorize qualities of self-discipline, tolerance, and a sense of mission. He describes those who simply teach in order to receive a salary, with no interest in the character formation of the students as "the blind leading the blind."

---

[72] Ibid., 51.

[73] Ibid., 16.

[74] Gülen, *Criteria, or Lights of the Way*, I, 36.

The lack of coordination or integration among competing and mutually antagonistic educational systems gave rise to what Gülen calls "a bitter struggle that should never have taken place: science versus religion."[75] This false dichotomy, which during the 19-20th Centuries exercised the energies of scholars, politicians, and religious leaders on both sides of the debate, resulted in a bifurcation of educational philosophies and methods. Modern secular educators saw religion as at best a useless expenditure of time and at worst an obstacle to progress. Among religious scholars, the debate led to a rejection of modernity and religion "as a political ideology rather than a religion in its true sense and function."[76] He feels that through an educational process in which religious scholars have a sound formation in the sciences and scientists are exposed to religious and spiritual values, that the "long religion-science conflict will come to an end, or at least its absurdity will be acknowledged."[77]

For this to come about, he asserts that a new style of education is necessary, one "that will fuse religious and scientific knowledge together with morality and spirituality, to produce genuinely enlightened people with hearts illumined by religious sciences and spirituality, minds illuminated with positive sciences," people dedicated to living according to humane qualities and moral values, who are also "cognizant of the socio-economic and political conditions of their time."[78] Having as a school's educational goal the integration of the study of science with character development, social awareness, and an active spirituality might appear to critics to be a highly idealistic, possibly quixotic, endeavor. The only adequate test of the feasibility of this educational philosophy is to examine how successful Mr. Gülen's associates have been

---

[75] Gülen, "The Necessity of Interfaith Dialogue: a Muslim Approach," 39.
[76] Ibid., 20.
[77] Ibid., 39.
[78] Ibid.

in establishing schools on these principles. I will return to the matter of verification later in this paper.

Several terms appear repeatedly in Gülen's writings on education and need to be clarified lest they cause misunderstanding. The first is that of *spirituality* and *spiritual values*. Some might read this as a code word for "religion" and employed to counteract prejudices towards religiosity in modern secular societies. However, it is clear that Gülen is using the term in a broader sense. For him, spirituality includes not only specifically religious teachings, but also ethics, logic, psychological health, and affective openness. Key terms in his writings are *compassion* and *tolerance*.[79] It is the task of education to instill such "non-quantifiable" qualities in students, in addition to training in the "exact" disciplines.

Other terms used frequently by Gülen need to be examined. He often speaks of the need for *cultural and traditional values*. His call for the introduction of cultural[80] and traditional[81] values in education has been interpreted by critics as a reactionary call to return to pre-Republican Ottoman society. He has consequently

---

[79] Gülen's studies of the life and mission of Muhammad focus repeatedly on the qualities of compassion and tolerance. M. Fethullah Gülen, *Prophet Muhammad as Commander*, 3-4, 7, 11, 87, 94, 100 *et passim*, and *Prophet Muhammad: the Infinite Light*, 3 volumes. Cf. I, 118-119-179 and II, 96, 123, 131, 150. At the 1999 Parliament of the World Religions held in Cape Town, South Africa, he stated: "The Prophet, upon him be peace and blessings, defined a true Muslim as one who harms no one with his or her words and actions, and who is the most trustworthy representative of universal peace," "The Necessity of Interfaith Dialogue: A Muslim approach."

[80] Cf., "Little attention and importance is given to the teaching of cultural values, although it is more necessary to education. If one day we are able to ensure that it is given importance, then we shall have reached a major objective." *Criteria or Lights of the Way*, I, 35.

[81] Cf., "Little attention and importance is given to the teaching of cultural values, although it is more necessary to education. If one day we are able to ensure that it is given importance, then we shall have reached a major objective." *Criteria or Lights of the Way*, I, 35.

been accused of being an *irticacı*, which might be translated in the Turkish context as "reactionary" or even "fundamentalist." This is an accusation which he has always denied. In defense of his position, he states:

> The word *irtica* means returning to the past or carrying the past to the present. I'm a person who's taken eternity as a goal, not only tomorrow. I'm thinking about our country's future and trying to do what I can about it. I've never had anything to do with taking my country backwards in any of my writings, spoken words or activities. But no one can label belief in God, worship, moral values and purporting matters unlimited by time as *irtica*.[82]

In proposing cultural and traditional values, he seems to regard Turkey's past as a long, slow accumulation of wisdom which still has much to teach modern people, and much in traditional wisdom is still quite relevant to the needs of today's societies. Because of this collected wisdom the past must not be discarded because of this collected wisdom. On the other hand, any attempts to reconstruct the past are both short-sighted and doomed to failure. One might say that while rejecting efforts to break with the Ottoman past, Gülen equally rejects efforts to reestablish or recreate pre-modern society.

The tendency among some modern reformers to "break free of the shackles of the past" he regards as a mixed blessing. Those elements of the heritage that were oppressive, stagnant, or had lost their original purpose and inspiration no doubt have to be superseded, but other, liberating and humanizing elements must be reaffirmed if new generations are going to be able to build a better future. The challenge today, he states, is "to evaluate the present conditions and make good use of the experience of past generations." It is clear that his thinking is not limited by internal debates about political directions in Turkey, nor even the

---

[82] Cited in Webb, 95.

future of Islamic societies. His educational vision is one that embraces societies "throughout the world" and the role of religious believers in shaping that world. He states:

> Along with the advances in science and technology, the last two or three centuries have witnessed, across the world, a break with traditional values and, in the name of renewal, attachment to different values and speculative fantasies. However, it is our hope, strengthened by promising developments all over the world, that the next century will be an age of belief and moral values, an age that will witness a renaissance and revival for believers throughout the world.[83]

His main interest in education is the future. He wants to form reformers, that is, those who, fortified with a value system that takes into account both the physical and non-materials aspects of humankind, can conceive and bring about the needed changes in society. Well-rounded education, by its very nature, must thus involve a personal transformation in the student. Students must be accompanied and encouraged to move out of restrictive, particularistic ways of thinking and to interiorize attitudes of self-control, self-discipline which will enable them to make a lasting contribution to society. He states:

> Those who attempt to reform the world must first reform themselves. In order for others to follow them on the way to a better world, they must purify their inner worlds of hatred, rancor, and jealousy, and adorn their outer worlds with all kinds of virtue. The utterances of those who are far removed from self-control and self-discipline, those who have failed to refine their feelings, may seem attractive and insightful at first, but they will not be able to inspire others—or, if indeed they can, the sentiments they arouse will soon die away.[84]

---

[83] Gülen, *Towards the Lost Paradise*, 103.
[84] Fethullah Gülen, Toward a Global Civilization of Love and Tolerance, 91.

To the extent that the crises in society are due to a lack of coordination among rival educational systems and philosophies, the new style of education proposed by Gülen is aimed at responding directly to the root causes of the crisis. In doing so, he claims, the new education offers a sound hope for building more stable and harmonious societies. As such, educational reform is a key to development and progress in nations. If national and private school systems are oriented solely towards the acquisition of material knowledge and mastery of technological skills, they cannot offer a way out of tensions and conflicts in society and offer a solution that can lay the basis of a better future. Calling for a type of education that seeks to develop both the material and spiritual needs of the students, Gülen sees educational reform as the key to positive societal change. He states: "The permanence of a nation depends upon the education of its people, upon their lives being guided to spiritual perfection. If nations have not been able to bring up well-rounded generations to whom they can entrust their future, then their future will be dark."[85]

Criticisms of Gülen's Educational Philosophy

Gülen's proposal of a new style of education, as put into practice in the network of schools associated with his name, has not been universally accepted, particularly in his native Turkey. Some critics have regarded the educational philosophy enunciated by Gülen as an intellectual cover for forming cadres who could conceivably pose a threat to the established secular order. Gülen has continually had to defend the schools from this type of criticism. They claim that by means of the many schools erected in Russia, Central Asia, the Caucasus, and the Balkans, Gülen is attempting to build a "Green Belt" around secular Turkey.

Any form of education which seeks to shape the feelings, values, and attitudes of students is likely to be accused of brainwash-

---

[85] Webb, 135.

ing. Mr. Gülen has not been spared this accusation. Critics in Turkey have claimed that even though there is no direct religious training carried out in the schools, religion and politically-oriented Islamic teaching are inculcated in the students by example and informal relations between students and teachers.

Gülen has responded to these accusations by noting that the schools established by his movement employ the program and curriculum of the Turkish Ministry of Education. He notes further that the schools are continually inspected, not only by the Turkish Education Ministry but also by the intelligence agencies in those countries where they have been established. Those who have inspected the schools have never found any evidence of brainwashing nor the inculcation of politically activist or anti-government sentiments, either through formal teaching or informal contact. By now, he states, the schools have been operating long enough that graduates are working in all sectors of Turkish society. They have never raised a complaint about undue influence being exerted on students, nor have official visitors make that claim:

> Two presidents of our country, premiers, ministers, members of parliament, scholars, high-ranking retired officers, journalists and thousands of others from every view and level have gone out and seen these schools and have returned. There has been no complaint of the kind referred to from the countries where the schools are found. Without exception, they mention them with praise.[86]

In the final analysis, the categories of "breaking with the past," "defending the past," or "restoring the past" are beside the point in attempting to understand Fethullah Gülen's educational vision. The schools inspired by his movement are conceived rather in terms of a humanism that is rooted in a particular historical context but is always aimed at transcending that context. Because of

---

[86]   Webb, 107.

the difference in context, the schools established in countries as diverse as Turkey, Kyrgyzstan, Denmark, or Brazil are necessarily very different from one another, but are all inspired by the same humanistic vision.

Gülen states this vision succinctly: "A person is truly human who learns and teaches and inspires others. It is difficult to regard as fully human someone who is ignorant and has no desire to learn. It is also questionable whether a learned person who does not renew and reform oneself so as to set an example for others is fully human." Into this humanistic vision fit the study of science, humanities, character development, and "spirituality" understood, as mentioned above, in the broad sense. It is thus not surprising that students of these schools have consistently scored high in university placement tests and produced champions in the International Knowledge Olympics in fields such as mathematics, physics, chemistry, and biology.

It is the concern for human formation, however, that distinguishes these schools from the thousands of other prep schools around the world. Gülen understands the school as a laboratory where students not only acquire information and skills, but where they can begin to ask questions about life, seek to understand the meaning of things, to begin to reflect on the particular contribution to life that they would like to make, and to understand life in this world in relation to the next. In some of his writings on education, he even speaks of the school in quasi-religious terms, as a holy place where sacred activities take place. He states:

> The school ... can shed light on vital ideas and events and enable its students to understand their natural and human environment. It can also quickly open the way to unveiling the meaning of things and events, which leads one to wholeness of thought and contemplation. In essence, the school is a kind of place of worship whose "holy persons" are teachers.[87]

---

[87] Fethullah Gülen, *Towards the Lost Paradise*, 98.

Gülen as a Teacher of Islam

The focus of this paper has been on Fethullah Gülen as an educator. His role as religious scholar and teacher (as underscored by the traditional honorific Hocaefendi) is a topic that deserves careful examination, as does the study of his religious thought as a modern interpreter of Islam. Such questions are outside the scope of this paper. However, because many of the accusations leveled against the educational ventures inspired by Mr. Gülen are due precisely to his accepted status as a scholar and teacher of Islam, a study of his educational vision would not be complete without a brief look at his writings on Islam.[88]

Of Gülen's more than 30 books, the majority deal with explicitly Islamic topics. Some are compilations of talks and sermons that he delivered to students and worshipers. Others are responses to questions put to him at one time or another by students. They range from studies of the biography of the Prophet Muhammad, to a basic introduction to Sufism, to a treatment of questions traditionally raised in the science of *kalam*, to elaborations of essential themes of Islamic faith. These studies are directed not toward specialists but at a more general audience of educated Muslims.[89]

---

[88] Two of these works have been translated into English: M. Fethullah Gülen, *Prophet Muhammad as Commander* and the two-volume work, *Prophet Muhammad: the Infinite Light*. Relying on sound *hadith* reports and the early *sira* or biography of Muhammad by Ibn Hisham, Gülen seeks mainly to outline the qualities displayed by Muhammad as a model to be imitated by modern Muslims.

[89] His work, *Key Concepts in the Practice of Sufism*, is a basic introduction to *tasawwuf* in which the author analyzes in turn each of the *maqamat* (stations) and *ahwal* (states) on the Sufi path. Gülen's *Asrın Getirdiği Tereddütler* is a wide-ranging work of four volumes, of which the first volume has been translated into English as *Questions This Modern Age Puts to Islam*. The work covers theological topics such as the revealed character of the Qur'an, the nature of revelation, and an interesting treatment of the possibility of the salvation of non-Muslims (149-160.)

In seeking to present the faith and practice of Islam in a way that responds to the needs of modern believers, Gülen can be said to carry forward the tradition of Bediüzzaman Said Nursi. Gülen's relationship to the Eastern Anatolian *shaykh* continues to be a matter of controversy in Turkey, where Said Nursi and his followers have remained under suspicion by the government in the decades before and after his death in 1960. Gülen has often been accused of being a *Nurcu*, that is, a follower of Said Nursi. Questioned about this accusation, Gülen does not deny that he has benefited from study the writings of Said Nursi, just has he has profited from reading the works of many other Muslim thinkers, but he does reject the claim that he is a follower of Nursi in any sectarian sense. He states:

> The word *Nurcu*, although it was used a little by Bediüzzaman Said Nursi, is basically used by his antagonists to belittle Nursi's movement and his followers and to be able to present it as a heterodox sect. In life, everyone benefits from and is influenced by many other people, writers, poets, and scholars. In my life I have read many historians and writers from the East and West, and I've benefitted from them. Bediüzzaman Said Nursi is only one of these. I never met him. On the other hand, I've never used suffixes like *-ci, -cu* [meaning –"ist"] that refer to a particular group. My only goal has been to live as a believer and to surrender my spirit to God as a believer.[90]

Nevertheless, some observers see the movement associated with Gülen as being one of the transformations that have occurred as Nursi's thought is continually reinterpreted and applied in evolving historical situations. Hakan Yavuz notes: "Some Turkish Nur-

---

Understanding and Belief: the Essentials of Islamic Faith takes up matters related to creation and causality, eschatology, the resurrection of the body, the unseen world of angels, *jinn*, and Satan, and concludes with a study of *nubuwwat*, the prophethood of Muhammad, and the question of science and religion in relation to the study of the Qur'an.

[90]   Cited in Webb, 96.

cus, such as Yeni Asya of Mehmet Kutlular and the Fethullah Gülen community, reimagined the movement as a 'Turkish Islam' and nationalized it." Yılmaz concurs: "Nursi's discourse 'has already weathered major economic, political, and educational transformations'... Today, the Hizmet Movement is a manifestation of this phenomenon. The movement spreads into daily life activities at two levels. First, it uses collective identity structures by producing meanings over time and history, reason and submission, love and worship, faith and rationale, science and revelation, divine being and natural order. At the second level the movement tries to influence major patterns of societal institutions, like high schools, foundations, university, insurance companies, finance houses, sport clubs, television and radio channels, newspapers and magazines."

What can be said about Fethullah Gülen's personal approach to interpreting the Islamic sources and tradition? The first thing that strikes the reader is his emphasis on morality and moral virtue, which he appears to stress as more central to the religious *élan* inspired by the Qur'an than ritual practice. While affirming the need for ritual, Gülen regards ethical uprightness as lying at the heart of the religious impulse. "Morality," he states, "is the essence of religion and a most fundamental portion of the Divine Message. If being virtuous and having good morals is to be heroic—and it is—the greatest heroes are, first, the Prophets and, after them, those who follow them in sincerity and devotion. A true Muslim is one who practices a truly universal, therefore Muslim, morality." He buttresses his point by citing a *hadith* from Muhammad in which he states: "Islam consists in good morals; I have been sent to perfect and complete good morals."

The various aspects of the Islamic way of life collectively known as the *sharia*, such as creed (*aqidah*), ritual obligations (*'ibadah*), economic affairs (*mu'amalat*), principles of government (*siyasah*), regulations of family file (*al-ahwal al-shakhsiyya*) and moral instruction (*akhlaq*), are all meant to work together to produce the honorable, ethically upright individual. In this broad sense of *islam* or submission of one's life to God, it can be said that the schools established by the movement associated with the name of Fethullah Gülen have as their inspiration an ethical vision that is rooted in Islam but is not limited in its expression to members of the *umma*. When Gülen speaks of forming students "dedicated to living according to humane qualities and moral values," who "adorn their outer world with all kinds of virtues," he is proposing a kind of universal ethical code that he as a Muslim has learned from Islam. It is equally obvious that he does not consider the virtues, humane qualities and moral values to be the exclusive possession of Muslims, as non-Muslim students are welcome in the schools and no attempt is made to proselytize.

With this strong ethical sense at the heart of his understanding of Islam, Gülen's many writings on the life of Muhammad affirm his role as Prophet who brought the Qur'anic revelation but emphasize even more strongly the figure of Muhammad as moral exemplar for Muslims, Muhammad as the first hearer of the Qur'an whose life was preeminently shaped by its message. Particularly in his two-volume work, *Prophet Muhammad: The Infinite Light*, Gülen's central concern would seem to be Muhammad as role model for the Muslim of today. This leads him to concentrate on the moral qualities of Muhammad manifested in personal relationships with his companions, wives, and enemies, and the qualities of leadership shown in being Commander of the Faithful. What Gülen seems to find of special importance in the life of Muhammad are personal qualities such as piety, sincerity, generosity, modesty, determination, truthfulness, compassion, patience, and tolerance, and leadership characteristics such as realism, courage, a sense of responsibility and farsightedness, and a readiness to consult, delegate, and forgive.

The religion of Islam is thus understood as a "way leading a person to perfection or enabling one to reacquire one's primordial angelic state." If Islam is seen as a path to moral perfection, one must consider the development of *tasawwuf* as a natural and inevitable development within the Islamic tradition. Gülen suggests an ethical definition of Sufism as "the continuous striving to be rid of all kinds of bad maxims and evil conduct and acquiring virtues." He praises the Sufis in Islamic history as being spiritual guides who have shown generations of Muslims how to follow this path to human perfection:

> [They] have illumined the way of people to the truth and trained them in the perfection of the self. Being the embodiments of sincerity, Divine love and purity of intention, the Sufi masters have become the motivating factor and source of power behind the Islamic conquests and the Islamization of conquered lands and peoples. Figures like Ghazali, Imam Rabbani and Bediüzzaman Said Nursi are the "revivers" or "renewers" of the highest degree, who combined in their persons both the enlightenment of sages, knowledge of religious scholars and spirituality of the greatest saints.[91]

Such a positive reading of the mystical Sufi tradition has inevitably led to accusations of his having created within his movement a type of neo-Sufi *tariqah*. While denying that he has ever been a member of a *tariqah*, much less that he has set up his own quasi-Sufi Order, Gülen asserts that to condemn Sufism, the spiritual dimension of Islam, is to tantamount to opposing the Islamic faith itself. He states:

> I have stated innumerable times that I'm not a member of a religious order. As a religion, Islam naturally emphasizes the spiritual realm. It takes the training of the ego as a basic principle. Asceticism, piety, kindness and sincerity are essential to it. In the history of Islam, the discipline that dwelt most on these matters was Sufism. Opposing this would be opposing the essence of Islam. But I repeat, just as I never joined a Sufi order, I have never had any relationship to one.[92]

---

[91] Fethullah Gülen, *Prophet Muhammad as Commander*, 122–123.
[92] Cited in Webb, 102–103.

Conclusion

Fethullah Gülen's educational vision can appear to be the sort of highly idealistic "mission statement" of the type that many educational projects have been declaring for more than a century. The real test remains whether the many schools associated with his movement, which have been consciously established on the basis of this idealism, have been successful in providing the kind of education advocated by Gülen. The answers will be as various as the expectations of those who evaluate these schools.[93] Some schools are likely to be more successful than others due to differences in the individual talents of teachers and administrators, in government support or interference, in financial arrangements, and in the capabilities and backgrounds of the students.

In quantifiable aspects of the educational process, such as generalized examinations, academic Olympics, and entrance into high-quality university programs, the schools in the "Gülen network" have largely verified the expectations of Fethullah Gülen and his associates. The schools, moreover, are greatly sought after by parents. For example, I visited a secondary school in Bishkek, Kyrgyzstan, in which 5000 applicants had sought entrance to a secondary school in which 250 places were available.

It is in the unquantifiable aspects of educational formation, precisely those which are meant to distinguish the schools in the Gülen network from the many other prep schools, that evaluation is most difficult and necessarily subjective. Have the schools been producing graduates who display "a marriage of mind and heart," as Gülen puts it, individuals of "thought, action, and inspiration"? Do the students who emerge from these schools go on to become "valiant young representatives of national thought and feeling"? Do they give evidence of the "profundity of ideas, clarity of thought, depth of feeling, cultural appreciation, and spiri-

---

[93] İhsan Yılmaz offers a very useful bibliography of recent studies on the thought of Fethullah Gülen. Please, see p. 148.

tual values" the instilling of which Gülen sees as one of the primary goals of education? It is the ongoing answers to such questions, which can only be given by graduates themselves and those who know and work with such graduates, which will form the ultimate criterion of evaluation by which the success of Gülen's educational philosophy can be judged.

Gülen's Pedagogy and the
Challenges for Modern Educators

Y ou may be acquainted with what, in my opinion, is one
of the most interesting phenomena occurring today in
the world of education. I am referring to those institutions usually referred to loosely as the "Gülen schools" or "schools
of the Hizmet Movement." These schools should not be thought of
as a type of centralized school system, but rather as a loose collection of independent schools created and operated according to
the pedagogical vision of the Turkish intellectual, Fethullah Gülen,
and frequently sharing human and material resources.

The actual number of schools is not known, even by members of the movement. These educational institutions were
founded by a circle of students, colleagues and businessmen
associated with Fethullah Gülen. The schools have been established by individual agreements between the countries in which
they are located and the educational foundations erected for this
purpose. Each school is an independently run institution, but
many of the schools rely on the services of Turkish companies to
provide educational supplies and human resources.

Gülen was born in eastern Anatolia in 1941. After a traditional Islamic education, he taught religion and served as imam, first
in his native region and then in the Mediterranean city of İzmir.
There he got involved in the formation of youth and became convinced of the need for a new kind of education in Turkey. He felt
that the existing educational alternatives were not offering youths
a genuine opportunity for holistic growth and personality development.

As a result of the polarization that took place in Turkish society in the 20th Century after the fall of the Ottoman Empire and the establishment of the Turkish Republic, competing and mutually antagonistic educational programs were put in place. These educational systems produced graduates who lacked an integrated perspective regarding the needs of society and who simply perpetuated existing ideological divisions. He states: "At a time when modern schools concentrated on ideological dogmas, institutions of religious education (*madrasas*) broke with life, institutions of spiritual training (*takyas*) were immersed in sheer metaphysics, and the army restricted itself to sheer force, this coordination was essentially not possible."

The secular schools erected in the era of the Turkish Republic were unable to free themselves of the prejudices and conventions of modernist ideology. At the same time, the *madrasas* that focused on instruction in the Islamic disciplines proved incapable of meeting the challenges of technology and scientific thought. They lack the flexibility, vision, and ability to break with past, enact change, and offer the type of educational formation that is needed in modern Turkey. The Sufi-oriented *takyas*, which traditionally had fostered the development of spiritual values, had lost their dynamism. As Gülen puts it, "they console themselves with virtues and wonders of the saints who had lived in previous centuries." The educational training offered by the military, which had in the Ottoman period represented religious energy and activity and been a symbol of national identity, degenerated into an assertion of attitudes of self-preservation.

The challenge that Gülen set for himself was to find a way in which these traditional pedagogical systems could move beyond regarding each other as rivals or enemies so that they could learn from one another. By integrating the insights and strengths found in the various educational currents, educators must seek, according to Gülen, to bring about a "marriage of mind and heart" if they hope to form individuals of "thought, action, and inspiration." An integration of the interior wisdom which is the cumulative heritage built up over the centuries with the scientific tools essential for the continued progress of the nation would enable students to move beyond the societal pressures of their environment and provide them with both internal stability and direction for their actions. He states: "Until we help them through education, the young will be captives of their environment. They wander aimlessly, intensely moved by their passions, but far from knowledge and reason. They can become truly valiant young representatives of national thought and feeling, provided their education integrates them with their past, and prepares them intelligently for the future."

This educational vision developed in response to the crises and needs of 20th Century Turkey. Until the opening up of Turkey to religiously-based ideas and projects in the time of Turgut Özal in the 1980's, Gülen's vision could only be put into practice in the dormitories or "lighthouses" he set up for high school and university students. The first schools were already operating in Turkey in 1989 when the Soviet Union was disbanded. Gülen's disciples immediately stepped into the post-communist educational vacuum and opened schools with Western-oriented curricula in the Russian Republic, throughout the Balkans, and in the newly independent nations of the Caucasus and Central Asia.

Opening new schools in the far-flung regions of the former Soviet Union forced Gülen and his colleagues to adapt the pedagogic principles that had originally been fashioned to meet the educational demands of modern Turkey to more universal and diverse educational needs and requirements. When, after the turn of the new century, schools began to be opened at an extraordinary rate in the far-flung reaches of Southeast Asia, Africa, Western Europe, and North and South America, there was an urgent need for some universal principles of education that were nevertheless flexible enough to be adapted to local situations and national laws and standards.

One of Gülen's principles that unite the effort of educators in various countries is his simultaneous respect for the past and eye toward the future. He states: "Integrate the [students] with their past, and prepare them intelligently for the future." This seemingly innocuous remark is, in the Turkish context, calling for a bold new direction in modern education, for one of the characteristic features of the Republic of Turkey has been its concerted effort to *break* with the Ottoman past. In the years since the establishment of the Turkish Republic, many Muslims have criticized government programs for uncritically adopting the best and worst of European civilization. They have seen secularization as not merely an unintended by-product of modernization, but rather as the conscious result of an anti-religious bias. The battle lines drawn up since the establishment of the Republic and reinforced by the mutually competitive systems of education have made the religious-secular debate one in which every scholar is expected to take a position.

One of the reasons why Gülen has been often attacked by both right and left, by secular and religious in Turkey is precisely because he has refused to take sides on an issue which he regards as a dead-end debate. He is instead proposing a future-oriented curriculum with which he hopes to move beyond the ongoing debate. Gülen's solution is to affirm the intended goal of modernization enacted by the Turkish Republic, but to show that a truly effective process of modernization must include the development of the whole person. In educational terms, it must take the major concerns of the various existing streams of education and weave them into a new educational style that will respond to changing demands of today's world.

This is very different from reactionary ideologies that seek to revive or restore the past. Denying that the education offered in the schools associated with his name is an attempt to restore the Ottoman system or to reinstate the caliphate, Gülen repeatedly affirms that the schools are oriented towards the future. However, despite the necessity of modernization, he holds, there are risks involved in any radical break with the past. Cut off from traditional values, young people are in danger of being educated with no values at all beyond those of material success. Non-material values such as profundity of ideas, clarity of thought, depth of feeling, cultural appreciation, or interest in spirituality tend to be ignored in modern educational practice which is too often aimed at mass-producing functionaries of a globalized market system.

Students emerging from such institutions might be adequately prepared to find jobs, but they will not have the necessary interior formation to achieve true human freedom. Leaders in both economic and political fields often favor and promote job-oriented, "value-free" education because it enables those with power to control more easily the "trained but not educated" working cadres. One writer has observed: "Gülen asserts that if you wish to keep masses under control, simply starve them in the area of knowledge. They can escape such tyranny only through education. The road to social justice is paved with adequate, universal education, for only this will give people sufficient understanding and tolerance to respect the rights of others." Thus, in Gülen's view, it is not only the establishment of justice which is hindered by the lack of well-rounded education, but also the recognition of human rights and attitudes of acceptance and tolerance toward others. If people are properly educated to think for themselves and to espouse the positive values of social justice, human rights and tolerance, they will be better prepared to be agents of change to implement these beneficial goals.

The crisis in modern societies arises from decades of schooling having produced, in Gülen's words, "generations with no ideals." It is human ideals, aims, goals, and vision that are the source of movement, action, and creativity in society. Those whose education has been limited to the acquisition of marketable skills are unable to produce the dynamism needed to inspire and carry out societal change. The result is social atrophy, decadence, and narcissism. He states: "When [people] are left with no ideals or aims, they become reduced to the condition of animated corpses, showing no signs of distinctively human life... Just as an inactive organ becomes atrophied and a tool which is not in use becomes rusty, so also aimless generations will eventually waste away because they lack ideals and aims."

The societal crisis is intensified by the fact that, in Gülen's judgment, the teachers and intelligentsia, who should be the guides and movers of society, have themselves become perpetuators of a restrictive and non-integrated approach to education. Rather than raising their voices in protest against the elimination of humane values from the educational system and campaigning for a pedagogy that integrates scientific preparation with non-material values studied in the disciplines of logic, ethics, culture, and spirituality, the educators themselves too often, as Gülen says, "readily adapted to the new low standard." He finds it difficult to understand how intellectuals could prefer the spiritually impoverished and technologically obsessed modern culture to a traditional cultural foundation that had grown in sophistication and subtlety down through the centuries.

It follows that if educational reform is to be accomplished, teacher training is a task that cannot be ignored. Gülen notes: "Education is different from teaching. Most human beings can be teachers, but the number of educators is severely limited." The difference between the two lies in that both teachers and educators impart information and teach skills, but the educator is one who has the ability to assist the students' personalities to emerge, who fosters thought and reflection, who builds character and enables the student to interiorize qualities of self-discipline, tolerance, and a sense of mission. He describes those who simply teach in order to receive a salary, with no interest in the character formation of the students as "the blind leading the blind."

The lack of coordination or integration among competing and mutually antagonistic educational systems gave rise to what Gülen calls "a bitter struggle that should never have taken place: science versus religion." This false dichotomy, which during the 19-20th Centuries exercised the energies of scholars, politicians, and religious leaders on both sides of the debate, resulted in a fragmentation in educational philosophies and methods. Modern secular educators saw religion as at best a useless expenditure of time and at worst an obstacle to progress. Among religious scholars, the debate led them to reject modernity as an anti-religious conspiracy and to view religion as a kind of social and political ideology. Gülen feels that through an educational process in which religious scholars have a sound formation in the sciences and scientists are exposed to religious and spiritual values, that the "long religion-science conflict will come to an end, or at least its absurdity will be acknowledged."

For this to come about, he asserts that a new style of education is necessary, one "that will fuse religious and scientific knowledge together with morality and spirituality, to produce genuinely enlightened people with hearts illumined by religious sciences and spirituality, minds illuminated with positive sciences," people dedicated to living according to humane qualities and moral values, who are also "cognizant of the socio-economic and political conditions of their time." Having as a school's educational goal the integration of the study of science with character development, social awareness, and an active spirituality might appear to critics to be a highly idealistic, possibly quixotic, endeavor. The only adequate test of the feasibility of this philosophy is to examine how successful Mr. Gülen's associates have been in establishing schools on these principles. I will return to the matter of verification later.

Several terms appear repeatedly in Gülen's writings need to be clarified lest they cause misunderstanding. The first is that of *spirituality* and *spiritual values*. Some might read this as a code word for "religion" which is used to counteract prejudices towards religiosity in secular societies. However, Gülen is using the term in a broader sense. For him, spirituality refers not only to specifically religious teachings, but also ethics, logic, psychological health, and affective openness. Key terms in his writings are *compassion* and *tolerance*. It is the task of education to instill such "non-quantifiable" qualities into the formation of students, over and above their training in the "exact" disciplines.

A second phrase often used by Gülen is what he terms the need for cultural and traditional values. His call for the introduction of cultural and traditional values in education has been interpreted by critics as a reactionary return to pre-Republican Ottoman society. He has consequently been accused of being an *irticacı*, which might be translated in the Turkish context as "reactionary" or even "fundamentalist," an accusation he has always denied.

In proposing cultural and traditional values, he regards the past as a long, slow accumulation of wisdom that still has much to teach modern people. Because of this collected wisdom the past must not be discarded. On the other hand, any attempts to reconstruct present societies on the model of the past are both short-sighted and doomed to failure. While rejecting efforts to break with the Ottoman past, Gülen equally rejects efforts to return to pre-modern society.

The tendency among some modern educators to "break free of the shackles of the past" Gülen regards as a mixed blessing. Those elements of the heritage that were oppressive, stagnant, or had lost their original purpose and inspiration no doubt have to be superseded, but liberating and humanizing elements in the tradition must be reaffirmed if new generations are going to be able to build a better future. The challenge today, he states, is "to evaluate the present conditions and make good use of the experience of past generations." His thinking is not limited by internal debates about political directions in Turkey, nor even the future of Islamic societies.

His educational vision shaped by his avowed religious commitment and he looks forward to a world renewed by the humane values enshrined in religious teaching. He sees this in terms of a religious renaissance. He states: "Along with advances in science and technology, the last centuries have witnessed around the world a break with traditional values and in the name of renewal attachment to different values and speculative fantasies. However, it is our hope that the next century will be an age of belief and moral values, an age that will witness a renaissance and revival for believers."

According to Gülen, education should be oriented toward forming reformers, that is, those who, fortified with a value system that takes into account both the physical and non-material aspects of humankind, can conceive and bring about the needed changes in society. Well-rounded education, by its very nature, must involve personal transformation in the student. Students must be encouraged to move out of restrictive, particularistic ways of thinking and to interiorize attitudes of self-control and self-discipline that will enable them to make a lasting contribution to society. He states: "Those who want to reform the world must first reform themselves. In order to bring others to the path of traveling to a better world, they must purify their inner worlds of hatred, rancor, and jealousy, and adorn their outer world with all kinds of virtues."

To the extent that the crises in society are due to a lack of coordination among rival educational systems and philosophies, the new style of education proposed by Gülen aims at responding to the root causes of the crisis. As such, educational reform is a key to development and progress in nations. If national and private school systems are oriented solely towards the acquisition of material knowledge and mastery of technological skills, they cannot offer a way out of tensions and conflicts in society and offer a solution that can lay the basis of a better future. In calling for a type of education that seeks to develop both the material and spiritual needs of the students, Gülen sees educational reform as the key to positive societal change.

The Wing of the Bird:
Gülen on Sincerity

Gülen as Spiritual Master

Much has been written about the thought of Fethullah Gülen in terms of the social programs and institutions inspired by his ideas. Some have studied his theory of education as the pedagogical basis for the schools and other educational ventures founded and administered by members of the community associated with Gülen's name. Others have focused on Gülen's vision as the philosophical motor behind a social movement working to produce social change and renewal, whether it be in Turkey, in the worldwide Islamic *umma*, or in the modern world in general. Still others have underlined Gülen's call for universal love, fellowship, and tolerance and consequently his encouragement of interreligious dialogue as an essentially Islamic obligation.

In this paper, I want to concentrate on another aspect of the thought of Fethullah Gülen, one that may prove, in the long run, to be the area of his greatest influence. This is his role as spiritual director and teacher of internalized Islamic virtue. It is the function Gülen plays as spiritual master whose counsel has guided individual Muslims and formed a coherent and workable community life among his disciples. Thousands of Turks, Central Asians, and others, ranging from students to businessmen to young professionals, look to Fethullah Gülen as their spiritual teacher whose advice and wisdom, rooted in the Islamic tradition, has shaped their understanding of the religion of Islam and has had a formative influence on their lives as Muslims in the modern world. This acknowledgement is manifest in the honorific title by which Gülen's disciples refer to him as "Hocaefendi," that is, "Respected Teacher."

This aspect of the teaching and counsel of Gülen has been often referred to as the "Sufi element" in his thought. The question of Gülen's relationship to the Sufi tradition has been much discussed by scholars and need be no more than noted here. According to Zeki Saritoprak, Gülen is "a Sufi in his own way."[94] Employing a term coined by Fazlur Rahman, I have referred to Gülen, and to Said Nursi before him, as "neo-Sufis," to describe their role as scholars who propose and explain Sufi concepts, but have not belonged to a *tariqah* or taken a *pir*.[95] Heon Kim terms Gülen's methodological principle "dialogic Sufism" or "humanitarian Sufism,"[96] while Rıfat Atay views Gülen as reviving the proto-Sufi *suffa* Tradition of studious piety which arose in Medina in the first centuries after Muhammad.[97]

Mustafa Gökçek notes that Gülen did not begin to write about Sufism until the 1990s, when he was over 50 years old.[98] His earlier sermons and writings focused mainly on basic elements of Islamic faith and moral prescriptions, although he often included examples from the lives of earlier Muslim mystics and ascetics. However, in 1990, Gülen began to include a brief insert in the

---

[94] Zeki Saritoprak, "Fethullah Gülen: A Sufi in His Own Way," 156-169.
[95] Thomas Michel, "Der türkische Islam im Dialog mit der modernen Gesellschaft. Die neo-sufistische Spiritualität der Gülen-Bewegung." See also, "Sufism and Modernity in the Thought of Fethullah Gülen," 341-353.
[96] Heon Kim, "Gülen's Dialogic Sufism: A Constructional and Constructive Factor of Dialogue," 374.
[97] Rıfat Atay, "Reviving the *Suffa* Tradition," 459-472.
[98] Mustafa Gökçek, "Fethullah Gülen and Sufism: a Historical Perspective."

magazine *Sızıntı* (*The Fountain*) that in each monthly issue elaborated a different concept of Sufi terminology. These were collected and became the basis for Gülen's masterwork, *Key Concepts in the Practice of Sufism*, which was published as two series or volumes in English.[99]

"Sincerity" in the Islamic Tradition

I do not intend to treat the whole gamut of the spiritual advice offered by Fethullah Gülen to his disciples, but instead I will focus on one central concept and try to show its role in maintaining a cohesive, Islamically-motivated community life. This is the Qur'anic concept of *ikhlas*, which is usually translated into English either as "purity of intention" or "sincerity." Both these translations touch on an essential aspect of the Qur'anic notion of *ikhlas*.

"Sincerity" usually indicates the notion of "honesty of mind" or "freedom from dissimulation or hypocrisy." A sincere person is one whose external words or deeds are in accord with their interior thoughts or feelings. A sincere person does not dissimulate or pretend to be expressing one thought or emotion while in reality his interior dispositions are to the contrary. Thus, a sincere person is not self-promoting, hypocritical, pretentious, two-faced, or devious. The sincere person neither flatters nor manipulates others. It is to this aspect of sincerity that Jesus exhorted his disciples in the Sermon on the Mount when he taught his disciples to say "yes" when they mean yes and "no" when they mean no (Matthew 5: 37).

However, there is another aspect of the Qur'anic notion of *ikhlas*. This notion, which brings together the notion of "purity" with that of "dedicating, devoting or consecrating oneself" to something, is a key virtue in Islamic practice.[100] *Ikhlas* is an eminently interior disposition by which the faithful Muslim should

---

[99] Fethullah Gülen, *Key Concepts in the Practice of Sufism I-II*.
[100] L. Gardet, *Encyclopaedia of Islam*, III: 1059.

perform all external actions a spirit of service and directed solely toward pleasing the Divine Lord. In Islam, the perfection of one's witness to faith can be gauged by the double standard of *ikhlas* (purity of intention) and *ihsan* (goodness).

It is noteworthy that the brief expression of the Islamic creed found in the Qur'anic chapter 116, "Say: He, Allah, is One. Allah is He on whom all depend. He begets not, nor is He begotten. And none is like Him," has been known in Islamic tradition as the Surah al-Ikhlas, that is, "The Chapter of Sincerity" or "The Chapter of Pure Religion."

The importance of *ikhlas* has been commented upon down through the centuries by Muslim scholars, exegetes, and spiritual guides in every generation. The Sufi masters have been particularly fond of elaborating on this virtue, to the extent that in the minds of many Muslims, *ikhlas* is considered a "Sufi concept." In commenting on *ikhlas*, Said Nursi must repeatedly distinguish his own advice from that of the teaching of the Sufis. While acknowledging the beneficial value of the instruction of the Sufi masters, he notes that "I am not a Sufi, but these principles of theirs make a good rule for our path."[101]

Nursi's approach differs from that of the Sufis because of his praxis-oriented approach, what he calls the "way of reality," in which he eschews contemplative speculation in favor of practical guidance for his disciples' life together. He states: "However, since our way is not the Sufi path but the way of reality, we are not compelled to perform this contemplation [of death] in an imaginary and hypothetical form like the Sufis."[102]

Because of its roots in the Qur'an and in the tradition of Islamic spiritual writing, Nursi's use of *ikhlas* can perhaps be more adequately conveyed in English by "purity of intention" or "pure religion" than simply by "sincerity." *Ikhlas* is when one practices

---

[101] Said Nursi, *Risale-i Nur*, The Twenty-first Flash, 216.
[102] Ibid., 217.

all the acts of religion solely for God's pleasure rather than for any personal benefit that may accrue to them, whether that be prestige, pride, or the admiration of others. When one "worships God with sincerity" one's intention is pure and undefiled by base or irrelevant motives. As the Qur'an states, "There is the type of man who gives his life to earn the pleasure of Allah: And Allah is full of kindness to (His) devotees" (Qur'an 2: 207).

The Wing of the Bird

While interpreting the basic meaning of the term to be "upright, sincere, and pure," Gülen indicates that *ikhlas* means "pursuing nothing worldly while worshiping and obeying God."[103] At the deepest level, sincerity can only be understood in the mystery of the relationship between God and God's faithful servant. Purity of intention is a grace or divine gift that God places in the heart of those He loves[104] in order to increase, deepen and give eternal value to the servant's ordinary good acts.

Gülen considers purity of intention to be one wing of a person's spiritual life before God. The other is faithfulness, and together the two virtues make up the pair of wings of divine grace that God implants in the soul, which enable a person to approach God directly without hindrance. He quotes Mawlana Jalaluddin Rumi to the effect that if good deeds were a body, purity of intention would be their soul. That is, it is a sincere intention that makes good deeds live, be effective, and have everlasting value. Without sincerity to animate deeds spiritually, all human endeavors would remain lifeless, ephemeral, and ultimately worthless. But those who fly with the two wings of sincerity and faithfulness will travel with God's protection and will unfailingly reach their destination, that is, "God's pleasure and approval."

---

[103] Fethullah Gülen, *Key Concepts in the Practice of Sufism*, 60.
[104] Ibid., 62.

Faithfulness, the other wing of the bird, enables God's servant to stick to his intention to serve God even when it is inconvenient or seemingly fruitless. This kind of loyalty to God is one of the most evident qualities of God's servants, an outstanding characteristic of all the prophets, and the source of wisdom in the believer. In the loyal, faithful servant, God will plant the seeds of wisdom that will then spring from that person's heart and tongue.

Gülen quotes Abu Yazid Bistami (Bayazid) to say that it is through sincere intention, not through human deeds, that a person goes to God. It is on the basis of a person's sincerity that God judges acts, not on the magnitude or notoriety of the deed. The size and quantity of good deeds is unimportant. Even a small deed or one that is unknown to others, if it is done with sincerity, is judged pleasing by God. Gülen notes that God rewards a small act done with purity of intention more highly than many more ostentatious deeds done without the sincere desire to serve God alone.

Just as the prophets could not take a step without sincerity, so also those who follow in the footsteps of the prophets will not be able to do anything without a pure intention. Gülen describes this purity of intention as "the pursuit of no worldly purpose in one's relationship with God."[105] In other words, worshiping and obeying God are the only reasons that a sincere person should have for performing any of their good actions.

Living with Purity of Intention

Like Said Nursi before him, Fethullah Gülen is not interested so much in being a theoretician of the spiritual life as in offering concrete, practical advice to those who come to him for spiritual counsel. In this way, Gülen, following Nursi, distinguishes himself from the great Sufi Masters like Al-Muhasibi, Al-Ghazali, and Hujwiri. Gülen is interested in continuing in the line of Nursi's

---

[105] Ibid., 60.

"path of reality," that of providing effective, helpful advice to Muslims who are seeking God's pleasure in this world.

Gülen advises his disciples to maintain spiritual discretion. In practical terms, if purity of intention means that the servant does everything solely to seek God's pleasure and for no worldly motive whatsoever, it follows that sincere believers should not be ostentatious in the good deeds they perform. One seeking God's pleasure alone should hide supererogatory acts from the view of others and remain silent about any edifying personal experiences, special treatment received from superiors, or special gifts with which one has been endowed by God.

There is much wisdom in this advice, given the universal human tendency to perform one's good deeds in order to be seen by others and gain their approval. Moreover, human motivation is often complex, with the desire to serve God mixed with a craving for human admiration and approval. The sincere servant recognizes that it is only God's approval, not that of other persons, that matters; thus it is unimportant whether or not one is seen to be serving God.

A person who does everything with purity of intention worries neither about being praised for his accomplishments nor censured for his failures. He does not care if others are aware or unaware of his achievements, nor is he preoccupied about receiving a reward. Such a person behaves with consistency, whether or not one is in public or in private.

Sincerity not only keeps one's intention pure, but also guards against pursuing one's goals with unworthy methods. Only purity of intention can insure that "the ends justify the means" will not become an Islamic principle. Gülen explains: "An Islamic goal can be achieved only through Islamic means and methods... Just as it is impossible to secure God's approval without sincerity and purity of intention, so, too, neither can Islam be served nor Muslims directed toward their real targets through diabolic means and methods."[106]

As a Christian, I am impressed how similar is this teaching on purity of intention to Jesus' words in the Sermon on the Mount that his disciples should do their good deeds only to please and obey God. He said, "When you give to the needy, do not let your left hand know what your right hand is doing, so that your giving may be in secret...And when you pray, go into your room, close the door and pray to your Father, who is unseen...When you fast, put oil on your head and wash your face, so that it will not be obvious to others that you are fasting, but only to your Father, who is unseen; and your Father, who sees what is done in secret, will reward you."

According to Gülen, sincerity teaches us that God's pleasure, not human recognition or respect, is the true goal of our acts of piety and goodness. Moreover, in sincere worship we discover that our human longing for Paradise is not a sufficient motivation for doing what is right. Speaking of worship, Gülen teaches: "Those performing [acts of worship] can be categorized by their intention, resolution, determination, and sincerity as follows: those who desire to enter Paradise, those who hope to be rescued from Hellfire, those who love and stand in awe of God, and those who feel that they must do so as a requirement of their relationship between God as the Creator and human beings."[107] The sincere worshiper no longer cares whether his deeds will form the basis for attaining Paradise, for he performs his duties with the sole intention of loving and serving God. Gülen cites the Second Century mystic Rabia bint al-Adawiyya, who stated: "O Lord, I swear by the beauty of nearness to You that I have not wor-

---

[106] Fethullah Gülen, "Towards the World of the Righteous Servants."
[107] Fethullah Gülen, *Toward a Global Civilization of Love and Tolerance*, 54.

shipped You either because of fear of Hell or out of the desire for Paradise. I have worshipped You because of You."[108]

In fact, sincerity should become second nature to God's servants, not a virtue after which a person consciously needs to strive. Gülen advises disciples to be "so involved in worship or religious deeds in seeking God's pleasure that one does not even remember whether one should be sincere or not."[109] In other words, even the virtue of sincerity itself must not be allowed to get in the way of pure service of God and become the final goal of religious observance. The only true objective in the performance of any good act is to serve and obey God and to thereby give God the pleasure and satisfaction that is due Him. For this reason, Gülen describes purity of intention as the first essential characteristic of Islamic piety.[110]

It is only the humble individual who can act with true sincerity. As Gülen explains: "Humble persons do not attribute fruits of work and efforts to themselves, nor do they regard their successes or efforts for God as making them superior to others. They do not care how others regard them; they do not demand a return for their services for God. They regard their being loved by others as a test of their sincerity, and do not exploit God's favors to them by boasting."[111]

To achieve this, the disciple must engage in self-examination and self-supervision. Only the person who has learned to be honest with oneself will be able to know whether one's motivation is solely to worship God or whether the true incentive that is being pursued is some worldly gain, such as self-satisfaction, human respect, or personal ambition. Thus, developing a habit of honest evaluation and reflection will enable a person to grow in purity of intention. Gülen calls this *muraqaba* (self-supervision), by which

---

[108] Fethullah Gülen, "*Ibada, Ubudiya*, and *Ubuda* (Worship, Servanthood, and Deep Devotion)."
[109] Fethullah Gülen, *Key Concepts in the Practice of Sufism*, 62.
[110] Fethullah Gülen, "*Taqwa* (Piety)."
[111] Fethullah Gülen, *Toward a Global Civilization of Love and Tolerance*, 80.

God's servants are led "to maintain the purity of thoughts, actions, and intentions even when they are alone, in the consciousness of His continual observation."[112]

It is not only for the purposes of an individual's spiritual growth that purity of intention is a key virtue among those who seek to do God's will. Purity of intention also has communitarian effects. There is nothing that can more quickly disrupt the proper bonds of friendship among disciples than personal ambition, competition, and rivalry. When a disciple is in the habit of calling attention to his superior abilities or achievements in one or another area, or to boast about his relationship to his superiors, resentment and jealousy will inevitably arise among his confreres.

In his emphasis on sincerity as a key element in preserving the unity of the community, Gülen's approach is very similar to that of Said Nursi, who repeatedly wrote of the necessity for sincerity to prevent disunity among the students of the *Risale-i Nur*. In his long discourses on sincerity, Nursi envisioned a community in which "Each of the members completes the deficiencies of the others, veils their faults, assists their needs, and helps them out in their duties."[113] If this type of relationship among fellow disciples is to be possible and the unity of the community is to be maintained, everyone must be sincerely striving solely to please God.

The history of many religious groups in various religions has shown repeatedly that it is jealousy, judgmentalness, and competition among members that is the cause of factionalism, resentment, and divisions into rival groups. The virtue of sincerity can combat these tendencies in two ways. Firstly, it is sincerity that enables God's servants to keep focused on serving God alone, thus making their actions, whether great or small, acceptable to God. Secondly, recognizing a fellow believer's sincerity can help a person to avoid carping criticism and summary condemnation

---

[112] Fethullah Gülen, *Key Concepts in the Practice of Sufism*, 57.
[113] Said Nursi, *Risale-i Nur*, The Twenty-first Flash, 214.

of a companion. Gülen teaches that those who seek God's blessing and strive to be true must cast no doubt on others' sincerity,
but should "value all servants of God as the greatest of people,
and appreciate each one as their peer. In their hearts, they dis-
solve any harshness or bad feelings coming from others, thus
showing how kindness defeats wrong."[114]

If Gülen has been able to instill a sense of harmony and united service (*hizmet*) among his followers, it is largely because of
the emphasis he has put on purity of intention. He cites Mawlana
Jalaluddin Rumi to this effect:

"You should be sincere in all your deeds,
So that the Majestic Lord may accept them
Sincerity is the wing of the bird of the acts of obedience
Without a wing, how can you fly to the abode of prosperity?"

---

[114] Fethullah Gülen, "An Ideal Society."

PART TWO

On the Hizmet
(Gülen) Movement

Introducing the
Hizmet Movement[115]

I thank the organizers for this invitation to be part of the inau-
gural dinner of the conference "Islam in the Age of Global
Challenges: Alternative Perspectives of the Gülen Movement." I am also grateful to Georgetown University for hosting
this event.

Many of you already know much about the life and thought
of Fethullah Gülen, but for those here who do not, allow me to
state a few words of introduction. I ask the indulgence of those
who in many cases know the Hizmet Movement (or the Gülen
Movement) much better than I. Mr. Gülen, affectionately known
as Hocaefendi or "Esteemed Teacher" by several million Muslims
who have been inspired and formed by his teaching, was born in
1938 in Eastern Turkey. After a traditional Islamic education,
Gülen began teaching religion and preaching in mosques, first in
Eastern Turkey and later in the Mediterranean city of İzmir. It
was in that modern, cosmopolitan environment that the Hizmet
Movement had its origins.

Gülen started out in what today we would call "youth ministry." By the 1970s, Gülen was lecturing in mosques, organizing
summer camps, and erecting "lighthouses" (dormitories for student formation) and slowly began to build a community of religiously motivated students. The importance that the lighthous-

---

[115] Delivered as keynote speech at the conference entitled "Islam in the Age
of Global Challenges: Alternative Perspectives of the Gülen Movement,"
November 14-15, 2008, Georgetown University, Washington, D.C.

es, residences, and study halls play to this day in the formation and cohesion of the movement must not be underestimated. There is no catalogue listing such residences, but reliable estimates put the number in the tens of thousands. In these centers of formation, the students not only supplement their secular high school and university studies or prepare for entrance exams, but they form friendships and a network of social relations. They also receive spiritual training through the study of the Qur'an and spiritual texts such as Said Nursi's *Risale-i Nur*, and they pursue their educational goals in a social environment free from the use of alcohol, drugs, tobacco, premarital sex, and violence.

As the community gradually began to take on its own identity and direction, its members, under Gülen's leadership, came to respond to a challenge put forward by Said Nursi, an influential 20th Century Muslim scholar. According to Nursi, the great threats to humankind in the modern era are three: ignorance, poverty, and disunity. Nursi called upon his disciples to combat these human tendencies that produce both destructive and self-destructive behavior in modern societies. Nursi taught that Muslims, in their struggle against these common enemies, should not try to go it alone but should form bonds of unity and cooperation with true Christians.

The genius of Fethullah Gülen has been to provide his community of disciples concrete, effective ways in which these ancient but still quite actual plagues can be resisted. The central notion of Gülen's teaching is "service," and Gülen has tried to form conscientious, dedicated Muslim social agents who will renew the Islamic community, and through it reshape modern society, on the bases of tolerance and love.

The first enemy noted by Said Nursi was that of *ignorance*. The Gülen community has tried to change society through a holistic pattern of education that draws from and integrates disparate strands of previous pedagogic systems. In the new social and economic climate that emerged in Turkey in the 1980s, during the presidency of Turgut Özal, the Hizmet Movement grew from involving a small number of students in a few cities like İzmir to become a huge educational endeavor with important business links. Although stemming from a broadly-conceived religious motivation, the so-called "Gülen" schools are not traditional Islamic schools, but secular institutions of high quality, as shown by the performances of students in science Olympiads, standardized comprehensive exams, and proficiency tests.

The community's educational commitment moved beyond its schools into the media with the publication of a daily newspaper, *Zaman*, and a television channel, Samanyolu and now publishes over 35 publications ranging from popular newsmagazines to professional journals. Here in the States, the Ebru cable television channel has full schedule of programming in English which seeks, according to their mission statement, "to educate, inspire and entertain viewers of all ages ...and to foster understanding through intercultural dialogue and mutual respect, thus promoting peace and diversity with our neighbors here and throughout the world."

After the fall of communism in the Soviet Union and Eastern Europe in 1989, the Gülen community was a key player in reconstructing post-Soviet education. Hundreds of schools and universities were set up throughout the former Soviet republics, both in the Russian Federated Republic, particularly in its predominantly Muslim regions, in the newly independent nations of the Caucasus and Central Asia, and in the Balkans. Television programs were made for the vast reaches of Central Asia, and scholarships were granted for study in Turkey.

The 21st Century saw a further expansion of the educational activities of the Gülen community as its activities moved beyond the boundaries of Muslim-majority regions into Western Europe, North and South America, Africa, and Southeast Asia.

An important but not exclusive focus was the education of migrants from Turkey and other Muslim countries. Here the pedagogic approach adapted to local needs. In many parts of Western Europe, the economic and bureaucratic difficulties of opening and supporting new schools often prevented this activity. The educational task became not so much one of competing with the existing national school systems, but that of ensuring that immigrant Turks and others would have an adequate educational background to be able to compete and succeed in state schools. Thus, in many parts of Western Europe, the Gülen community's educational efforts have focused on weekend classes and tutorials aimed at supplementing the instruction given in the state schools and at preparing for standardized exams.

In the charter schools associated with the movement in the United States, located often in areas with a high concentration of Turkish-Americans, the challenge has been to provide an opportunity for students to attain a high level of academic achievement. Schools run by the Hizmet Movement have been among the most highly awarded, particularly in scientific fields, in states like New Jersey and Texas. These are not "Islamic schools" in that even though their inspiration is found in enlightened Islamic ideals, both the teaching and administrative staff and the student body are made up of Muslims and also followers of other religions.

The most recent estimates point to more than 1000 schools and universities in 140 countries on five continents. The schools do not form a centralized "school system." Each is established and run by individual members of the Gülen community in a privately registered and funded foundation. The teachers receive a common spiritual training and are sent to where the need is considered the greatest, but there is no central governing board that issues instructions on educational policy, curriculum, or discipline. Each school is "twinned" with a particular city or region in Turkey, where businessmen sympathetic to the movement undertake financial responsibility for the school until such time that it can be self-supporting.

Aspects of the Gülen community's educational projects will be one of the themes of our upcoming conference. The second great enemy to be faced, according to Nursi, is *poverty*. Several papers (including my own) will deal with the aid, welfare, and development aspects of movement. Many of these projects, which have grown exponentially in the past decade, are summed up under the heading of *"Kimse yok mu?"*, a Turkish phrase which may be translated: "Doesn't anyone out there care?"

Finally, the third enemy of modern people, according to Said Nursi, is *disunity*. Hatred and suspicion, generalization and stereotyping, rivalry and name-calling across religious, ethnic, and racial lines have divided people and led to tensions and even violence in society. To bring people together, members of the Hizmet Movement have set up dialogue institutes and associations in the States, Turkey and elsewhere in Europe, Africa and Asia. In the United States, almost every major city and college town now has one of these dialogue associations, which function analogously to the Rumi Forum here in Washington. By providing lecture series, organizing trips to Turkey, and offering *iftar* dinners during the month of Ramadan, the community hopes to bridge the boundaries of religion and culture and build friendship and unity.

Already in the 1930s, Said Nursi called for "Muslim-Christian unity" to oppose godless tendencies in modern societies. Gülen goes beyond Nursi's appeal in two important respects. Firstly, Muslims should seek unity not only with "good Christians," as Nursi had proposed, but with the conscientious followers of all religions. The active participation of Jewish and Christian representatives at the Abrahamic symposia sponsored by the movement show the members' sincerity in their desire to dialogue and cooperate with all believers. Secondly, for Gülen the motivation for this dialogue is not simply a strategic alliance to oppose secularizing tendencies in modern life, but is demanded by Islamic faith itself. He said in 1999:

The goal of dialogue among world religions is not simply to destroy the materialistic world view that has caused such harm. Rather, the very nature of religion demands this dialogue. Judaism, Christianity, and Islam, and even Hinduism and Buddhism pursue the same goal. As a Muslim, I accept all Prophets and Books sent to different peoples throughout history, and regard belief in them as an essential principle of being Muslim.[116]

In short, the dialogue projects of the community, like its educational ventures and its efforts at poverty alleviation, are oriented towards serving the common good of humanity and building a better, more peaceful future. If the source of this vision is Qur'anic, it is not narrowly sectarian. I conclude with Gülen's words taken from one of his recent books:

> I believe and hope that the world of the new millennium will be a happier, more just, and more compassionate place, contrary to the fears of some people. Islam, Christianity, and Judaism all stem from the same root; all have essentially the same basic beliefs, and are nourished from the same source. Although they have lived as rival religions for centuries, the common points between them and their shared responsibility to build a happy world for all of the creatures of God make interfaith dialogue among them necessary. This dialogue has now expanded to include the religions of Asia and other areas. The results have been positive.[117]

I hope that you can see from this brief introduction why the thought of Fethullah Gülen and the achievements of the community of his disciples are worth our study and reflection during the forthcoming conference. Thank you.

---

[116] Fethullah Gülen, Capetown, 1999, p. 14.
[117] Fethullah Gülen, *Toward a Global Civilization of Love and Tolerance*, 231.

Identifying Our
Partners in Dialogue

Finding Partners for Dialogue

Many people see the need for interreligious and intercultural dialogue but are not sure where to begin. I have often been asked, "How do you go about starting up dialogue with others?" Especially because I am a Christian who has lived and shared life with Muslims for many years, they ask, "How do you go about beginning a dialogue with Muslims? Where do you start?"

It's a good question and one that I found myself asking back in 1978 in Indonesia. I had just finished my graduate studies in Islamic thought and had returned to Indonesia. I was wondering where to begin to meet Muslims and enter into dialogue with them. On one occasion, I asked a prominent Muslim scholar how to go about this. The wisdom of his answer has stayed with me and proven itself true over the years, so that by now it has also become my answer.

He told me that the first thing we have to do is to look around at the society in which we live to try to identify those who are our logical partners in dialogue. Who are the individuals and groups with whom we find ourselves sharing ideals, whose vision of the future is most compatible with our own, whose value system intersects with ours at various points? Thus, for the Christian who wants to enter into dialogue with Muslims, the first step is to distinguish and recognize the movements, organizations and communities of Muslims who are open to dialogue with us, who have something to say to us from which we might learn something, and who are also ready to listen to us, to hear our stories, and to appreciate our religious and humane vision of life, even as they remain committed to their own spiritual path.

The Hizmet Movement:
A Good Partner in Dialogue

One of the Muslim movements with whom I have found much common understanding is what is often called "the Hizmet Movement." This is a community of Muslims inspired by the thought of M. Fethullah Gülen, a Turkish scholar and educator. Mr. Gülen has denied that he has any movement of his own, but describes the movement rather as one of like-minded colleagues and students who share a common vision and commitment to society. I came to know this community back in the 1990s through a close friend of mine, Msgr. George Marovitch, who was secretary of the Catholic Bishops' Conference of Turkey. Over the years, I have met many members of this movement, and I have grown in respect for who they are and what they are seeking to do in society. It is about this movement that I would like to speak to you today.

To understand this movement, it is necessary to know a bit of the background and spiritual journey of the founder. Fethullah Gülen was born and educated in the far eastern region of Turkey. He began his career as a teacher of religion and preacher in the mosques. In 1958, at the age of 20, Gülen became aware of the writings of Said Nursi, which had a formative influence upon his thinking. Like many other Turkish Muslims, Gülen began to study the *Risale-i Nur*, Said Nursi's voluminous (6000 page) commentary on the Qur'an.

Gülen became a teacher of Qur'anic studies in the Mediterranean city of İzmir, and it was in that modern, cosmopolitan environment that the movement had its origins. In the 1970s, by means of lecturing in mosques, organizing summer camps, and erecting "lighthouses" (dormitories for student formation), Gülen began to build a community of religiously motivated students trained both in the Islamic and secular sciences.

The importance that the lighthouses (*ışık evler*), residences (*yurts*), and study halls (*dershanes*) play until today in the formation and cohesion of the movement must not be underestimated. Students not only supplement their secular high school studies and prepare for university entrance examinations, but they form friendships and a network of social relations, receive spiritual training through the study of the Qur'an and the *Risale-i Nur*, and pursue their educational goals in a social environment free from the use of alcohol, drugs, tobacco, premarital sex, and violence.

Gülen gave a socially-oriented thrust to religious commitment. Gülen taught the need to transform society through generous service. In Gülen's vision it is the social effect of conscientious, dedicated, committed Muslim social agents that is the key to renewal of Islamic life. Gülen hopes to form Muslims who will be tolerant and open-minded, who can build peace with others, and who are ready to serve others through education, development, and dialogue.

Hizmet Schools: A new Pedagogy

Members of the Hizmet community hope to change society through a new type of education that draws from and integrates disparate strands of previous pedagogic systems. Gülen's starting point was his recognition of the need for a new kind of school, a system of education that would draw what was best from the existing alternatives and integrate them into the kind of education needed by modern students. Gülen looked at the kinds of education that were being offered in Turkey in his day, He found that each had some strong point, but that each was also lacking in some important aspect of education.

He felt that that the secular state schools were unable to free themselves of the prejudices and conventions of modernist ideology. On the other hand, the *madrasas* have limited their efforts to transmitting the religious sciences but have shown little interest or capability to meet the challenges of technology and scientific thought. As a result, the *madrasas* lack the flexibility, vision, and ability to break with past, enact change, and offer the type of educational formation that is needed today. The Sufi-oriented *takyas*, which traditionally had placed the emphasis on the development of spiritual values, lost their dynamism. Finally, the educational training offered by the military, which had in previous ages been a symbol of national identity and religious energy and activity, deteriorated into an inflexible program aimed at self-assertion and self-preservation.

The challenge today, as Gülen see it, is to find a way in which these traditional pedagogical systems can overcome the tendency to regard each other as rivals or enemies, so that they can begin to work together and learn from one another. By integrating the insights and strengths found in the various educational currents, educators must seek to bring about a "marriage of mind and heart" if they hope to form individuals of "thought, action, and inspiration." Integration of the interior wisdom which is the cumulative heritage accumulated over the centuries with the scientific tools essential for the continued progress of the nation will enable students to move beyond the societal pressures of their environment and provide them with both internal stability and direction for their actions. He states:

> Until we help them through education, the young will be captives of their environment. They wander aimlessly, intensely moved by their passions, but far from knowledge and reason. They can become truly valiant young representatives of national thought and feeling, provided their education integrates them with their past, and prepares them intelligently for the future.[118]

---

[118] Fethullah Gülen, *Criteria or Lights of the Way*, I: 59.

From Turkish Student Initiative to International Movement

In the new social and economic climate that emerged in Turkey during the presidency of Turgut Özal, the Hizmet movement grew from involving a small number of students in a few cities like İzmir to become a huge educational endeavor with important business and political links. Although stemming from a broadly-conceived religious motivation, the schools are not traditional "Islamic" schools, but secular institutions of high quality, as shown by the winning performances of students in science Olympiads and the like.

In the 1980s, the community brought its commitment to education beyond its schools and moved into the media with the publication of a daily newspaper, *Zaman*, and a television channel, Samanyolu. Today *Zaman* is published in 20 countries with an average circulation of a half-million. In all, about 35 newspapers and magazines in various languages are projects of the Hizmet community.

After the fall of communism in the Soviet Union and Eastern Europe in 1989, the Gülen community was a key player in filling the gap in the post-Soviet educational systems. Hundreds of schools and universities were set up throughout the former Soviet republics, both in Russia, particularly in predominantly Muslim regions, in the newly independent nations of the Caucasus and Central Asia, and in Balkans states like Albania, Macedonia, Bosnia, Moldova, Bulgaria and Kosovo. Television programs were prepared which were destined to be aired in the vast reaches of Central Asia, and scholarships were granted for study in Turkey.

The new century saw a further expansion of the educational activities of the Gülen community as it moved beyond the boundaries of Muslim-majority regions into China, Western Europe, North and South America, Africa, and Southeast Asia. The primary but not exclusive focus was on educating migrants from Turkey and other Muslim countries. Here the pedagogic approach underwent some adaptation. In many parts of Western Europe, the economic and bureaucratic difficulties of opening and supporting new schools discouraged and often prevented this activity. Moreover, in these regions, the movement often encountered a level of education of high quality. The educational task became not so much one of competing with the existing national public school systems, but that of ensuring that immigrant Turks and others would have an adequate educational background to be able to compete and succeed in the government schools. Thus, in many parts of Western Europe, the Gülen community in its educational efforts has focused on weekend classes and tutorials aimed at supplementing the instruction given in the state schools and at preparing for standardized exams.

In the schools associated with the movement in the United States, the challenge has been to provide an opportunity for students to attain a high level of academic achievement. In fact, particularly in scientific fields, in states like New Jersey and Texas, schools run by members of the Hizmet movement have been among the most highly awarded. These are not "Islamic schools" in that even though the inspiration for the schools is found in enlightened Islamic ideals, both the teaching and administrative staff and the student body are made up of the followers of other religions as well as of Muslims. In some cases, religious instruction is offered once a week, while in other cases religion is not taught in the schools.

The schools do not form a centralized "school system." Each school is established and run by individual members of the Gülen community in a privately registered and funded foundation. The teachers receive a common spiritual training and are sent to wherever the need is considered the greatest, but there is no central governing board that sends out instructions on educational policy, curriculum, or discipline. Rather, each school is "twinned" with a particular city or region in Turkey, which undertakes financial responsibility for the new school.

Gülen's genius does not lie so much in reinterpreting the teaching of the Qur'an as in applying traditional Islamic prescriptions in entirely new ways to respond to constantly changing social needs. According to the Albanian scholar Bekim Agai: "The key point for Gülen is that the Islamic principles are unchanging, and yet must be given concrete form in each new era. Once, a Qur'an course might have been the best way to invest Islamic donations, but [today] other Islamic activities take precedence. He succeeds in gaining support in conservative Islamic circles for new Islamic fields of action by using traditional Islamic terminology and defining his terms conventionally, but at the same time furnishing them with innovative implications for the present day. He argues that questions of morality and education are more essential for today's Islam than are political issues, and that present-day Muslims are confronted with entirely different problems than the question of whether or not to introduce the *sharia*."[119]

Commitment to Dialogue

Gülen's reading of the needs of today's world has led him and his movement to put interreligious dialogue at the center of their concerns. In his speech in 1999 at the Parliament of the World's Religions, Gülen presented an optimistic vision of interreligious harmony. "It is my conviction that in the future years, the new millennium will witness unprecedented religious blooming and the followers of world religions, such as Muslims, Christians, Jews, Buddhists, Hindus and others, will walk hand-in-hand to build a promised bright future of the world."

Gülen believes that the duty of Muslims to work for dialogue and unity should not be limited to Christians, but is to be extend-

---

[119] "A Modern Turkish-Islamic Reformist," en.qantara.de/content/portrait-of-fethullah-gulen-a-modern-turkish-islamic-reformist

ed to the conscientious followers of all religions. Secondly, the motivation for this dialogue is not simply a strategic alliance to oppose atheistic and secularizing tendencies in modern life, but is called for by the nature of Islamic belief itself. Gülen stated: "The very nature of religion demands this dialogue. Judaism, Christianity, and Islam, and even Hinduism and Buddhism pursue the same goal. As a Muslim, I accept all Prophets and Books sent to different peoples throughout history, and regard belief in them as an essential principle of being Muslim."[120]

To further its pursuits of interreligious dialogue, the Hizmet movement has been active in sponsoring and organizing "Abrahamic" dialogues with high-ranking representatives of Judaism, Christianity, and Islam. The movement also organizes associations for the promotion of interreligious activities at the local and regional level, and has established dialogue associations in Africa, Europe, North and South America, and Asia, all of which take independent initiatives toward promoting interreligious understanding and cooperation.

I conclude by returning to my original idea. The first step in dialogue is to identify those individuals, groups, and movements in society with whom we can speak and with whom we can work for the good of all. I suggest that Christians in Africa, as in Europe and America, those interested in dialogue with Muslims could not do better at the present time than to regard the Hizmet community inspired by the teaching of Fethullah Gülen as a movement in which they will find suitable and enriching dialogue partners.

---

[120] Fethullah Gülen, Capetown, 1999, p. 14.

Fethullah Gülen and His Movement: Friends or Foes?

I think that some, or even most of you, already know quite a bit about Fethullah Gülen and the movement associated with his name. On the other hand, some of you may have very little acquaintance with the man and his ideas. In this short paper, I hope to say something worthwhile about Mr. Gülen without annoying the former with information they already know or mystifying the latter by presuming too much. At the beginning I should say a word about the approach that I am going to take. I think that I have read most of the literature that has been written about Gülen and the movement, both by members and outside scholars, but given the fact that for more than 20 years now I have known Mr. Gülen personally and have followed his movement and taken part in their various activities, I will try to take a personal rather than strictly academic approach to this topic.

Since I first met Fethullah Gülen in the late 1980s, I have watched his movement grow from a local student movement in the city of İzmir to become a controversial national phenomenon with powerful social, economic and political significance for Turkey. In later years we've seen further transformation into what the movement has become today, an international force for educational and spiritual renewal among Muslims, and perhaps the Muslim organization most committed to dialogue with people of other faiths.

My first encounter with Gülen came about like this. While I was teaching an introduction to Christian theology in Ankara in 1986, I was introduced to the writings of Said Nursi, who was probably the most influential Muslim thinker in Turkey in the 20th Century. Nursi, whose thinking evolved from political and social activism to a kind of contemplative study of the Qur'an, continues to have millions of followers. Sociologists estimate those who regularly study Nursi's 6000-page commentary on the Qur'an to be between 8-13 million. For example, in Ankara, where I was living, I was told that there are over 90 groups that meet weekly to study the *Risale-i Nur*, as Nursi's writings are called. I've participated often in their *sohbets*, which could be described as faith-sharing sessions. These weekly sessions seem to be especially attractive to professional groups like doctors, engineers, university professors and, in Ankara, civil servants in the various government ministries.

In 1986, not much of the *Risale-i Nur* or "Message of Light," had been translated into English or Arabic. But through my students at Ankara's Theology Faculty I came to know those portions of the *Risale* that had been translated. I began to read and discuss Nursi's writings together with my students and with ordinary Muslim believers.

Various ideas of Said Nursi I found very attractive. Nursi held that devout Muslims and Christians should be united in professing divine values in a world that was threatened by aggressive atheism. Secondly, he believed that the days of "*jihad* of the sword" are over, and the only appropriate jihad for modern times is "jihad of the word," or persuasion, rational argument, personal witness. Thirdly, Nursi held that the real enemies of Muslims were not this or that group of people, but rather that the common enemies of all humankind were three: ignorance, poverty, and disunity. I felt that these and similar views could form a sound basis for dialogue and cooperation in pursuing the common mission that Vatican II envisioned for Christians and Muslims, that of working together for the good of all to build peace, establish social justice, defend moral values, and promote human freedom.

In 1988, I was invited to give a talk at the *Risale-i Nur* international symposium in İstanbul and speak on Muslim-Christian unity according to the *Risale-i Nur*. It was a huge gathering, with about 3000 persons in attendance. After the talk, some young people invited me to come and meet their "shaykh" or *hoca*, and that was the first time I met Fethullah Gülen. At the time, I had never heard of Gülen or his still localized movement, but I was impressed by the esteem in which he was held by the youths, who crowded around him to hear what he had to say.

Two years later, at the next symposium, we met again and he invited me to his home in a suburb of İstanbul, where we had a long discussion on matters of Christian and Islamic faith. Since that time, we meet regularly, usually at his home in the Pennsylvania hills in the USA, whenever the occasion arises.

My involvement over the years with both the Nur community of followers of Said Nursi and the Hizmet *cemaat* inspired by the ideas of Fethullah Gülen was not simply my personal initiative, but strongly encouraged by the Turkish bishops. Over 20 years ago the bishops urged me to associate with these communities because they represent "the tolerant, pluralist, pro-minority elements in Turkish Muslim society."

To understand the development of Gülen's ideas, it is important to note that in his teens he came to know and was greatly influenced by the writings of Said Nursi. Nursi believed that the Islamic community would only be renewed as an instrument for combating the enemies of ignorance, poverty, and disunity once enough Muslims had been personally transformed by the study of his Qur'an commentary. Gülen accepted Nursi's analysis of the "true enemies of Islam and humankind," but he broke with the traditional communities of *Risale-i Nur* students in his conviction that the evils of ignorance, poverty, and disunity could only be opposed by the creation of effective institutions.

He began his work in the 1970s as an *imam* and *khatib* in the Mediterranean city of İzmir. Much of his time was devoted to the formation of youth. He conducted classes in Arabic and the Qur'an, organized summer camps for students, and set up *ışık evler* (lighthouses) as residences where high school and university students could pursue their studies and at the same time undergo spiritual and character formation.

From this beginning, Gülen came to the conclusion that the key to the renewal of Islamic societies was educational reform. The existing options in Turkey at that time all emphasized some pedagogical elements while ignoring others. In the state schools one might receive an adequate grounding in the sciences, but delivered with a suspicion and even antagonism towards religion. The military schools emphasized discipline and responsibility, but neglected questions of ethics and character formation. The *madrasas* offered a solid background in Islamic sciences, but failed to prepare students to take up positions of leadership in society. Still less the Sufi *takyas*, which emphasized spirituality but had degenerated academically to the point of focusing almost entirely on pious and inspirational tales.

Gülen became convinced of the need for a new, holistic educational model that would draw from the strength of each of the traditional types of school and would respond to the actual needs of Islamic societies. It wasn't until the liberalism introduced in the 1980s by Turgut Özal that it was possible for Gülen and his colleagues to open the first schools based on his pedagogical vision. By 1989, when the Soviet Union disbanded, the Hizmet community had already opened and operated several schools in Turkey; they quickly responded to the call in the former Soviet Union for schools with a Western-oriented curriculum. The schools were immediately popular in the Muslim-majority regions of the vast Soviet empire; in places like the Balkans and Caucasus where Muslims were in the minority, the schools offered quality modern education in a system with values that Muslim parents could trust.

After the turn of the century, schools were opened in Southeast Asia, Western Europe, and in North and South America. Today, for example, there are about 220 schools in Africa and over 200 in the United States. In former communist countries like Kyrgyzstan and Albania with relatively small populations, there are over 25 schools in each. In addition, the community has set up about twelve universities, mainly in Turkey, in the Caucasus, and in the Central Asian republics. Because of the high quality of education and English-language curriculum, the schools tend to attract the elite. The tuition is usually quite high, although on an average, 20-30% of the students are on scholarships.

The community's commitment to education is not limited to the traditional understanding of what constitutes a school. The community also runs highly successful *dershaneler*, (literally, "study halls"). These are college preparatory courses aimed at helping students to perform well on the national college entrance exams. (For example, in Ankara where I was living, 22,000 students are studying in these supplementary education programs.) To promote mass education, the community has set up television stations and publishes highly successful newspapers and more than 50 popular magazines and professional journals.

Recently, Gülen has been encouraging special institutions for the education of the poor. Again I take the example of Ankara, where there are now over 45 *okuma salonları*, i.e. "reading salons." These are tuition-free schools for the poorest children in slum areas. In İstanbul and in southeast Turkey there are many times that number. Along with well-qualified, mainly volunteer Turkish instructors, I have taught English in these education centers as a form of social service.

The importance that the lighthouses, residences (*yurts*), and study halls play to this day in the formation and cohesion of the movement must not be underestimated. There is no catalogue listing such residences, but reliable estimates are in the tens of thousands. In these centers of formation, the students not only supplement their secular high school studies and prepare for university entrance examinations, but they also form friendships and a network of social relations. They receive spiritual training through the study of the *Qur'an* and the *Risale-i Nur* and pursue their educational goals in a social environment free from the use of alcohol, drugs, smoking, premarital sex, and violence. It is not surprising that the residents of these dormitories tend to achieve higher test scores than students living elsewhere.

The schools do not form a centralized "school system." Each is established and run by individual members of the Gülen community in a privately funded foundation. The teachers receive a common spiritual training and are sent to where the need is considered the greatest, but there is no central governing board that sends out instructions on educational policy, curriculum, or discipline. Rather, each school is "twinned" with a particular city or region in Turkey, where businessmen sympathetic to the movement undertake financial responsibility for the new school.

A story taken from my personal experience in Turkey can help to explain the ways the schools are funded. In 2002, I was in Urfa giving some lectures on Christian theology to the students of Harran University's Islamic theological faculty. One evening, I was invited by some friends who belonged to the Hizmet Movement to a dinner that was to be held for local businessmen who served as benefactors of the movement. As it happened, the man I was sitting next to owned a plumbing supplies company. We were speaking of various things, and I mentioned that I spend quite a bit of time in Southeast Asia. He surprised me by asking, "Have you been to Cambodia?" I said, "Yes, it happens I was there last year for a Muslim-Christian meeting." He said, quite simply, "I have a school in Kampong Cham."

Actually, I know the Turkish school in Cambodia established by members of the Gülen community. It offers excellent education to Cambodian students irrespective of religion – the great majority are Buddhists, but also a few Muslims and Christians. But I never expected to meet the principal donor who made the school possible in a plumbing supplies businessman from an ancient city of Eastern Anatolia. This is an unexpected example of globalization. Fifty years ago, Urfa and Phnom Penh might as well have been on different planets. Today they have been linked through the efforts of this Islamic movement. I had similar experiences visiting the movement's schools in Kyrgyzstan, East Africa, Indonesia, Philippines, and the United States, as well as meeting donors from all parts of Turkey.

In 2002, to combat poverty, the community set up its own relief and development organization named *Kimse Yok Mu*. What began as an emergency relief program to care for earthquake and flood victims in Turkey has now grown to an aid and economic development agency working in 55 countries with an annual operating budget of $52 million dollars. In 2010, over a quarter-million people were fed during Ramadan at soup kitchens set up throughout Asia, Africa, and the Middle East.

One of the areas by which the Gülen community is best known among non-Muslims is their effort to combat disunity by working to promote interreligious dialogue. There is probably no international organization, of any religious background, that has made a greater investment of human, physical, and monetary resources aimed at building interfaith understanding and harmony. The community has set up dialogue centers in Turkey, Europe, Australia, the Americas, Southeast Asia, throughout Africa. In the USA alone, there are more than 200 such centers that promote dialogue through *iftar* dinners, lecture series, trips to Turkey, academic conferences, visits to places of worship and celebrations of feast days of various religions.

Their dialogue associations focus on specific groups like students, women's groups, professionals, and journalists. Their "intra-Muslim" dialogues (e.g., Sunni-Alevi, Turk-Kurd, and secular-religious in Turkey, Kurd-Arab-Turkmen in Iraq, Tausug-Maranao in the Philippines) after a slow start, are now showing some success in overcoming past tensions and conflicts. Reflecting upon my years at the Pontifical Council for Interreligious Dialogue in the

Vatican, I find the Gülen community today creating institutions and putting into practice programs for interfaith harmony that our Church teachings had long been calling for.

Although each of these projects is the result of individual initiatives, the inspiration for all this comes from the preaching and writings of Mr. Gülen, whose weekly radio broadcasts are still widely heard, discussed, and recorded for future repetition. As such, the particular approach that Gülen takes toward the Qur'an and Islamic tradition is worth our attention.

The key Qur'anic concepts upon which Gülen bases his spiritual instruction are two: *ikhlas*, or purity of intention, and *'ibadah*, or worship. These concepts are neither unique nor original to Gülen; both have a long history in Islamic discourse, particularly that of the Sufis. In his appropriation of these concepts and the centrality which he gives to them in his own teaching, Gülen shows the strong influence that the writings of Said Nursi have had on his own thought.

In the Islamic tradition, *ikhlas* brings together the notion of "purity" with that of "dedicating, devoting or consecrating oneself" to something. It is the eminently interior disposition by which the faithful Muslim performs all external actions in a spirit of service directed solely toward pleasing the Divine Lord. The importance of *ikhlas* has been commented upon down through the centuries by Muslim scholars, exegetes, and spiritual guides in every generation.

For Gülen, *ikhlas* means "pursuing nothing worldly while worshiping and obeying God." At the deepest level, sincerity can only be understood in the mystery of the relationship between God and God's faithful servant. Purity of intention is a grace or divine gift that God places in the heart of those He loves in order to increase, deepen and give eternal value to the servant's ordinary good acts.

Gülen teaches that purity of intention is what makes good deeds live, be effective, and have everlasting value. Unless deeds are animated by a sincere intention of serving God, all human endeavors would remain lifeless, ephemeral, and ultimately worthless. Gülen quotes Abu Yazid Bistami (Bayazid) to say that it is through purity of intention, not through human deeds, that a person goes to God. It is on the basis of a person's sincerity that God judges acts, not on the magnitude or notoriety of the deed. Thus, the size and quantity of good deeds is unimportant. Even a small deed or one that is unknown to others, if it is done with sincerity, is judged by God more highly than more ostentatious deeds done without the sincere desire to serve God alone.

The implications for the members of the members of the Gülen community are obvious: activities which are themselves trivial—preparing a meal for guests, picking up visitors at the airport, cleaning up after an *iftar*, volunteer teaching of poor children—all have the value of religious acts if they are done with a pure intention, that of worshiping God. This broad concept of worship ties *ikhlas* to Gülen's second key concept, that of *'ibadah*, or servanthood.

Derived from the Arabic root meaning slave or servant, *'ibadah* carries the idea of enslaving oneself to God or of acting as God's servant, with the consequent connotations of obedience, submission, devotion, faithfulness, service etc. The concept is not an innovation within the Abrahamic tradition, and is well known in both the Hebrew Scriptures and the Christian New Testament. It has received due attention in the writings of Christian and Jewish spiritual authors.

However, in many treatments of Islamic belief and practice, and in the minds of many Muslim believers, *'ibadah* is simply equated with ritual acts, specifically the ritual practices such as the Daily Prayers (*Salah*), the Ramadan fast, the pilgrimage to Mecca etc., that are obligatory for all Muslims. Gülen expands upon this traditional view of *'ibadah* to define it very broadly as "fulfilling God's commands in one's daily life, and fulfilling the obligations of being God's servant." It is interesting to note that there is no specific reference to ritual performance in this definition. In Gülen's view, servanthood goes far beyond ritual performance to include everything that one does to live and act according to God's will. When a member of the community leaves home to go and teach physics in a high school in Kazakhstan, he is performing 'ibadah; he is worshiping God. When a businessman donates funds so that schools, dialogue centers, well-digging projects, and publishing houses can be founded and maintained, he is doing 'ibadah. His donations are a form of divine worship.

Gülen's comprehensive understanding of worship has resulted almost in a kind of sacralization of education and helps to account for the emphasis the movement has given to opening and operating schools. As an example, I offer this passage from one of Gülen's writings on education. "A school is a place of learning, where everything related to this life and the next is taught. It can shed light on vital ideas and events, and enable students to understand their natural and human environment. A school can also open the way to unveiling the meaning of things and events, thereby leading a student to wholeness of thought and contemplation. In essence, a school is a kind of place of worship; the 'holy leaders' are the teachers."[6]

The broad compass that Gülen gives to 'ibadah is meant to have an integrating effect in the lives of his followers. The far-reaching notion of servanthood enables the members of the movement to bring together and maintain in equilibrium their devotional life, vocational commitment, and communitarian responsibilities. However, to play this integrative role in the life of a believer, "worship" must embrace the totality of attitudes and actions of service.

Worship has not only an integrative but also a liberative role in the believer's life. An attitude of worship enables the believer to arrive at true freedom by becoming free from the obstacles to freedom, escape from the self-imposed dungeon people have created for themselves and the multifarious forms of slavery to which humans subject themselves. Gülen puts it as follows: "If worship is the placing of a consciousness of being bound to God into one's heart, if it is the liberation of one's self from all types of slavery, if it is the title of seeing, hearing, and feeling the beauty, order, and harmony that belong to Him in every molecule of existence, then worship is the most immediate way to turn our face to God."

Like the Sufi writers before him, Gülen distinguishes between the various stages or levels of *'ibadah*. Whereas the first stage bears the connotation of "living in the consciousness of being God's servant," a deeper level, in Arabic *'ubudiyyah,* means "fulfilling God's commands in one's daily life." In other words, *'ibadah* refers to what the devout believer must do to serve and obey God in daily life, and *'ubudiyyah* indicates the attitude which the believer must take towards God, the object of worship.

Finally, once again reaching back to the Sufi tradition, Gülen notes a still deeper stage of worshipful involvement, that of "devotion," or *'ubudah*. Just as the Sufi teachers spoke of *'ibadah* as the service performed by ordinary believers striving to advance on the path to God and described *'ubudiyyah* as the servanthood of those advanced souls whose mental and spiritual attitudes enable them to overcome seemingly insurmountable obstacles, *'ubudah* is the deep devotion of those who live with a profound awareness of God's presence even in the most banal of daily activities.

Gülen cites Ibn al-Farid to affirm the superiority of this final stage of devotion: "The acts of worship and duties of servanthood required by every station or rank that I have reached during my spiritual journey have been fulfilled by my devotion." However, for the Sufis, *'ubudah* was a rare state of soul (*hal*) achieved by advanced practitioners on the Sufi path. Gülen characteristically orients even the stage of *'ubudah* toward those members of the *cemaat* engaged in what he sees to be the mission of Islam in the world, that is, service of God by serving others. He affirms: "This vital mission can only be realized by the devout and godly, who never think of themselves, except insofar as they see their own salvation through the salvation of others."

Gülen puts much hope in this "new generation" of idealistic young Muslims. "The future will be the work of these devout young people who can represent such a significant mission, showing their responsibility and exhibiting their accomplishments. The existence and continuance of our nation and the nations related to us will be permeated with the thoughts, inspirations and outcomes of a new civilization and with the vast, reviving dynamism of a rich culture, carried into the future on the shoulders of these devout youths. They are the trustees of the sublime truths and the heirs of our historical riches."

In my opinion, if one wants to find in summary the kind of Muslim that Gülen is trying to form, one need not look further than to study what Gülen has written on the twin concepts of *ikhlas* and *'ibadah*. The genius of Gülen, in my view, lies not so much the originality of his ideas, nor in his ability to organize social projects, which he has wisely left to others, but it lies in his talent as an Islamic preacher who can inspire young people to both heroic and hidden lives of selfless service and can equally motivate successful businessmen and professionals to support financially the community's projects of service.

To the question posed in the title of this talk, "Are Gülen and the Hizmet community friends or foes?" I must answer that they are our friends. They are the kind of Muslim interlocutors for an active dialogue for which we have been searching since the time of Nostra Aetate.

The Hizmet Community
and the Jesuits: Some Points
of Comparison

The topic that I will speak about today is that of the Gülen community and the Jesuits, and I am asked to note some points of comparison. I should mention at the beginning that two scholars have already independently treated this topic.

One of these studies has already been published. It is the paper prepared by Michael David Graskemper, a young American scholar at Harvard University in the United States, and was delivered at the international conference, "Muslim World in Transition: Contributions of the Gülen Movement," that was held in London at the London School of Economics on 25-27 October 2007. Mr. Graskemper's paper was entitled "A Bridge to Interreligious Cooperation: the Gülen-Jesuit Educational Nexus."

The other paper was prepared by Dr. Patrick Howell, a Jesuit professor at Seattle University in the United States. Dr. Howell's paper has been accepted by the conference "East-West Encounters: the Hizmet Movement," which is scheduled to be held at the University of Southern California on 4-6 December of this year. Dr. Howell's paper is entitled "Dialogue between Jesuit and Gülen Educational and Spiritual Foundations."

Both papers focus on the educational philosophy and activities of the two movements. Today I will aim at taking up the more general topic and being more broadly informative.

If I were giving this talk in the United States, I would feel that I should begin by introducing the audience to the background and works of the Hizmet Movement, and I could presume that the participants already knew much about the Jesuits. Here in İstanbul, the opposite is true; I believe that you are all well-informed, probably better than me, about the Hizmet Movement, but I should offer some background information on who the Jesuits are and what they do.

The Jesuits are a Catholic religious order founded about 470 years ago in 1541. The proper name of the community is "The Society of Jesus," and the name "Jesuit," which was originally disparaging, stuck and is today the usual name for the community. The Jesuits were inspired by the life and writings of Ignatius of Loyola, a Spanish soldier who underwent a deep spiritual conversion and devoted the rest of his life to the service of God. Ignatius lived at the time of the Protestant Reformation when many people were leaving the Catholic Church to join the Protestants. The Protestant reformers believed that the Catholic Church was too corrupt and wanted to found new "reformed" Churches, but Ignatius and his companions worked to renew and reform the Catholic Church from within and to invite nominal Christians to a deeper, transformed commitment to their faith.

Ignatius proposed two main instruments of renewal: spiritual development and education. To bring about spiritual transformation, the Jesuits founded throughout Europe "retreat houses," that is, places for prayer and spiritual renewal. All Jesuits must undergo 30 days of "spiritual exercises" twice during their lives, as well as 8 days of spiritual renewal every year.

The second instrument of renewal was education. They founded schools and universities in every major city of Europe, as well as North and South America, Asia, and Africa. In the United States, for example, there are 28 Jesuit universities and over 40 high schools, 5 universities in the Philippines, 8 in Brazil etc., and in India, there are over 100,000 students in Jesuit schools of higher education. Graskemper notes that "at the core of this project lies a determination to make education not just a commodity for the privileged, but a powerful tool for transforming society."

In this vision that education is about more than simply communicating information, we can find an appropriate opening to a comparison with the schools of the Hizmet Movement. Gülen, like Ignatius, has a broader vision than simply to run a school system. He wants to change the world and make it a better, more just and peaceful place. He wants to serve society by producing a new generation of students who are well prepared scientifically, and who are instilled with the ideals to use their educational preparation for the common good, rather than for their own selfish comfort.

Compare this vision of Gülen with the mission statement of Georgetown University, the Jesuit university in Washington, D.C. This was the earliest Jesuit university in the United States, dating back to 1789, and has produced many of the academic, political, religious, and economic leaders of the United States. Georgetown's mission statement reads as follows:

"Georgetown seeks to be a place where:

1. *understanding* is joined to *commitment*,
2. where the search for *truth* is informed by a sense of *responsibility* for society,
3. where *academic excellence* in teaching is joined with the cultivation of *virtue*,
4. and where a *community* is formed which sustains men and women in their education and their conviction that life is only lived well when it is lived generously in the *service* of others."

Those involved in schools produced by the Hizmet will recognize the four key elements of this mission that are not foreign to their own pedagogical vision:

1. Understanding is linked to engagement in society; knowledge is not simply for self-interest or aggrandizement, it is for serving society.

2. Search for truth brings with it a sense of responsibility for others.

3. Academic scholarship must go hand-in-hand with moral values and personal transformation.

4. Finally, education seeks to create a community of people who share the view that life is lived best when people are serving others.

There is also a common conviction between those involved in Hizmet and the men and women who follow an Ignatian spirituality that God is to be encountered and served in the carrying out of their daily duties. If one is a math teacher, one serves God best by being a conscientious, well-prepared, loving math teacher. It is a this-world spirituality, emphasizing service and commitment. In both Hizmet and Jesuit schools, the notion of education is holistic. There is an awareness that much education goes on outside the classroom, and that the teachers' role is as much that of role model as it is a provider of information. The Jesuit concept of *cura personalis* is mirrored in the Hizmet schools by a personal approach to the student, a concern for the family, visits to the home and colloquia with the parents and, when it is appropriate, with the extended family.

A strong point of comparison is the fact that both Ignatius and Gülen were innovators in education. They looked at the existing possibilities of education and found them wanting. The societies in which they lived needed something new. In the time of Ignatius, the sons of pious aristocratic families were sent to monastic schools to learn a bit of Latin, philosophy, theology, rhetoric, and law. At the same time, the university tradition stemming from places like Paris, Bologna, and Salamanca offered a secular education, strong in sciences and medicine, but strongly influenced by Renaissance humanism and often strongly critical of religion and religious values. In the time of Ignatius, the views of the Protestant reformers, especially those of John Calvin, were making headway in the European universities.

Ignatius saw a need for a new kind of school, on that would be the equal of the secular universities in scientific education, but would also concentrate on character development and the ability to discern truth in arguments and debates. The goal of Jesuit education has been described as "teaching the student to think"; in other words, education goes beyond simply filling the students' minds with information. It should make them critical and take well-founded positions in regard to truth.

Note the similarities with the educational philosophy expressed by Fethullah Gülen. Describing the educational situation in Turkey in the latter half of the 20th Century, he states: "At a time when modern schools concentrated on ideological dogmas, institutions of religious education (*madrasas*) broke with life, institutions of spiritual training (*takyas*) were immersed in sheer metaphysics, and the army restricted itself to sheer force, this [educational] coordination was essentially not possible." Gülen saw that it was not simply a question of opening a new school, but that a new *type* of school was necessary. By integrating the insights and strengths found in the various educational currents, he held, educators must seek to bring about a "marriage of mind and heart" if they hope to form individuals of "thought, action, and inspiration."

An important element of comparison between the Hizmet schools and those of the Jesuits are their essentially decentralized nature. In neither case can we speak accurately of a "Hizmet school system" or a "Jesuit school system." Gülen stated once that he is tired of repeating that he does not "have" any schools. Rather, people who have been influenced by his educational and social vision have looked at the local needs and started their own schools that are fashioned to respond to the needs of the local society.

The curriculum is to a great extent determined by national directives, but local prerogatives determine the school's priorities. For example, in the highly conflictual environment of tensions and violence between Christian and Muslim in the southern Philippines, the Hizmet school in Zamboanga is entitled The

Philippine-Turkish School of Tolerance," and the school sees itself as a laboratory for Muslim and Christian students learning to live together in peace and harmony. I should add that the Jesuit university in the same city, the Ateneo de Zamboanga, shares the same vision of providing an atmosphere of respect and tolerance for Muslims and Christians, and cooperates with the Hizmet school in many projects. For example, prospective teachers at the Hizmet school perfect their knowledge of English at the Jesuit school.

In his paper, Howell sees three main points of convergence between Ignatius and Gülen:

1. their mystical and religious roots,
2. emphasis on experience and pragmatic *action*, rather than retreat from daily life;
3. and their devotion to building up *community*.

I have already addressed the second and third points of Howell's observation, but the first point might need some elaboration. Fethullah Gülen in his writings draws upon the broad-minded, tolerant exponents of the Turkish Sufi tradition to be spiritual models for modern Muslims. The Sufis have, he states, "illumined the way of people to the truth and trained them in the perfection of the self...Figures like Ghazali, Imam Rabbani and Bediüzzaman Said Nursi are the "revivers" or "renewers" of the highest degree, who combined in their persons both the enlightenment of sages, knowledge of religious scholars and spirituality of the greatest saints." He often cites Jalaluddin Rumi, Ahmad Yasawi, and Yunus Emre in order to teach elements of spirituality. Similarly, Ignatius was not simply a theoretician but a mystic who drew upon his experiential encounters with God to give direction and strength to his commitment to follow and serve Jesus Christ.

Gülen's approach to Islam emphasizes the moral or ethical aspect over that of dry ritual. He also sees morality as the universal aspect of the Islamic message. Gülen states: "Morality is the essence of religion and a most fundamental portion of the Divine

Message. If being virtuous and having good morals is to be hero-ic—and it is—the greatest heroes are, first, the Prophets and, after them, those who follow them in sincerity and devotion. A true Muslim is one who practices a truly universal, therefore Muslim, morality.

Similarly, Ignatius consistently emphasized the importance of ethics over theological speculation. His spirituality has been described as "voluntarist," that is, focused on the will, rather than "rationalist," centered on the intellect. The concept of "doing God's will in all things" is central to his understanding of the Christian message. For the past 470 years, the motto of the Jesuits has been *Ad majorem Dei gloriam*, that is, to do every-thing "for the greater glory of God. This is a spiritual ideal quite similar to Gülen's emphasis on *ikhlas* or pure intention, which means doing everything, great or small, solely with the intention of pleasing God. Thus, at the heart of Jesuit spirituality we find the deepest point of convergence with the Islamic understand-ing that Fethullah Gülen has sought to convey to Hizmet mem-bers. It is not surprising that this common ideal is often lived out in very similar life styles.

The Hizmet Movement: Its Contribution at a Time of Global Tensions

I t has become a cliché to say that we live in an age of globalization. It is more difficult to see how this reality impacts upon a religious movement like that of Fethullah Gülen. The phenomenon of globalization provides us with stories both inspiring and brutal. I thought that I would begin with one of each, to set the stage for looking at the contribution being made by the modern Muslim movement associated with the name of Fethullah Gülen.

The first story is an experience I had a few years ago in the city of Urfa in Turkey. Urfa is an ancient city in eastern Anatolia with a long and distinguished past. The city is called "the city of the prophets," connected with the figures of Abraham, Job, Shuayb (the Biblical Jethro) and Elisha and revered as the birthplace of Abraham. Busloads of pilgrims arrive daily from all parts of Turkey, Syria, and Iran to pay homage to Khalil, God's intimate friend. As Edessa, the city was once one of the great early centers of Christianity in the Middle East, and later on, the center of the scientific and philosophical community of Sabaeans, who had so much influence on the subsequent development of Islamic thought. The modern city is especially fascinating for a foreign visitor like myself, for Urfa is the crossroads of three great Middle Eastern civilizations, and its population is approximately ⅓ Turkish, ⅓ Arab, and ⅓ Kurd.

In 2002, I was in Urfa giving some lectures on Christian theology to the students of Harran University's Islamic theological faculty. One evening I was invited by some friends who belonged to the movement of Fethullah Gülen to a dinner that was to be held for some of the local businessmen who acted as benefactors of the movement. As it happened, the man I was sitting next to owned a plumbing supplies company. We were speaking of various things, and I mentioned that I spend quite a bit of time in Southeast Asia. He surprised me by asking, "Have you been to Cambodia?" I said, "Yes, it happens I was there last year for a Muslim-Christian meeting." He said, quite simply, "I have a school in Kampong Cham."

Actually, I know the Turkish school in Cambodia established by members of the Gülen community. It offers excellent education to Cambodian students irrespective of religion—there are Buddhists, Muslims, Hindus, and Christians in the school—but I never expected to meet the principal donor who made the school possible in a plumbing supplies businessman from an ancient city of Eastern Anatolia. This is truly globalization. Fifty years ago, Urfa and Phnom Penh might as well have been on different planets. Today they have been linked through the efforts of this Islamic movement.

The other example of globalization is disturbing rather than uplifting. Anyone who has been following the news knows the tensions that we are experiencing at the moment between Christians and Muslims in many parts of the world in the aftermath of those Danish cartoons about the prophet Muhammad. The latest count of Muslims murdered by Christians in Onitsha, Nigeria is 135, following upon 40-50 Christians killed earlier by Muslims in northern Nigeria in previous weeks. After an Italian minister wore a t-shirt emblazoned with the offensive cartoon, another 11 persons died in riots outside the Italian consulate in Benghazi, Libya. Violence has also erupted also in widely-distant countries like Pakistan, Indonesia, Lebanon, and Afghanistan. It is truly a modern example of globalization that scurrilous cartoons can be published in one country, and innocent people who perhaps had never seen the cartoons or even knew that they existed could be murdered continents away.

It is not my intention here to speak about the cartoons. You are all as aware as I of the reports and analyses that have been appearing almost daily in newspapers and journals, on television and radio talk shows. My point is that events such as those which occurred in Nigeria, as well as the avalanche of information, commentary, and speculation that surrounds and gives new emotive life to any event that takes place anywhere, is another aspect of globalization in which we all, whether we like it or not, are forced to operate.

My topic for this evening is the spiritual and educational movement associated with the name of Fethullah Gülen and the contribution that the members of this movement are making to Muslim-Christian harmony in the midst of today's tense and sometimes violent climate. I know that many of you are already well acquainted with this movement, but probably some of you do not know the movement very well. Let me begin with a bit of background and ask the indulgence of those who in some cases know the movement of Fethullah Gülen and his associates much better than I.

Fethullah Gülen was born and educated in the city of Erzurum in eastern Anatolia in Turkey. He started out as a religion teacher and preacher in the mosques, first in Eastern Anatolia and then in İzmir. In 1958, at the age of 20, Gülen came to know the writings of Said Nursi, and this had a formative influence upon his thinking. Said Nursi was a 20th-Century Muslim scholar whose 6000-page commentary on the Qur'an, the *Risale-i Nur*, has influenced the lives and practice of millions of modern Muslims. According to Hakan Yavuz: "[Gülen's acquaintance with Nursi's writings] facilitated his shift from a particular localized Islamic identity and community to a more cosmopolitan and discursive understanding of Islam. Nursi's writings empowered him to engage with diverse epistemological systems."

Gülen became a teacher of Qur'an studies in the Mediterranean city of İzmir, and in that modern, cosmopolitan environment the movement associated with his name had its origins. In the 1970s, Gülen was lecturing in mosques, organizing summer camps, and erecting "lighthouses" (dormitories for student formation) and slowly began to build a community of religiously motivated students trained both in the Islamic and secular sciences.

The importance that the lighthouses, residences (yurts), and study halls (dershanes) play to this day in the formation and cohesion of the movement must not be underestimated. There is no catalogue listing such residences, but reliable estimates are in the tens of thousands. In these centers of formation, the students not only supplement their secular high school studies and prepare for university entrance examinations, but they form friendships and a network of social relations, and also receive spiritual training through the study of the Qur'an and the *Risale-i Nur* and pursue their educational goals in a social environment free from the use of alcohol, drugs, smoking, premarital sex, and violence.

The Gülen community gradually began to take on an identity and direction distinct from the *Risale-i Nur* movement, as Gülen himself produced new *ijtihad*s which distinguished the community from that of the original students of the *Risale-i Nur*. Nursi had focused on personal renewal of the Muslim through the study of the Qur'an and wanted to help the modern believer move beyond the dichotomies found in Turkish society of his day through a spiritual transformation that would come about by the study of the *Risale-i Nur*.

By contrast, for Gülen and the community associated with his name, personal transformation is secondary to social transformation. Both thinkers, Nursi and Gülen, are seeking to reform and reshape society. Nursi puts the emphasis on the individual Muslim who must be changed through an enlightened encounter with the Qur'an in the *Risale-i Nur*, while Gülen has a vision of conscientious, dedicated, committed Muslim social agents who will renew the Islamic community and through it reshape modern society on the bases of tolerance and love. Whereas for Nursi the key term is "study," the central idea of Gülen is "service." Members of the Gülen community hope to change society through a holistic pattern of education that draws from and integrates disparate strands of previous pedagogic systems. Although Nursi was already aware of the limitations of traditional systems of education available to Muslims in Turkey, it was Gülen and his movement that gave time and energy toward working out an effective alternative.

In the new social and economic climate that emerged in Turkey during the presidency of Turgut Özal, the Hizmet Movement grew from involving a small number of students in a few cities like İzmir to become a huge educational endeavor with important business and political links. Although stemming from a broadly-conceived religious motivation, the schools are not traditional "Islamic" schools, but secular institutions of high quality, as shown by the performances of students in science olympiads and standardized comprehensive exams and proficiency tests. In the 1980s, the community moved beyond its schools into the media with the publication of a daily newspaper, *Zaman*, and a television channel, Samanyolu and now publishes over 35 publications ranging from popular newsmagazines to professional journals.

After the fall of communism in the Soviet Union and Eastern Europe in 1989, the Gülen community was a key player in reconstructing post-Soviet education. Hundreds of schools and universities were set up throughout the former Soviet republics, both within the Russian Federated Republic—particularly in its predominantly Muslim regions such as Tatarstan, Yakutia, and Chechnya—, in the newly independent nations of the Caucasus and Central Asia, and in the predominantly Muslim and pluralist regions of the Balkans such as Albania, Macedonia, Bosnia, Moldova, Bulgaria and Kosovo. Television programs were prepared which were destined to be aired in the vast reaches of Central Asia, and scholarships were granted for study in Turkey.

The 21st Century saw a further expansion of the educational activities of the Gülen community as it moved beyond the boundaries of Muslim-majority regions into China, Western Europe, North and South America, Africa, and Southeast Asia. An important but not exclusive focus was the education of migrants from Turkey and other Muslim countries. Here the pedagogic approach adapted to local needs. In many parts of Western Europe, the economic and bureaucratic difficulties of opening and supporting new schools often prevented this activity.

Moreover, in these regions, the movement usually encountered a level of education of high quality. The educational task became not so much one of competing with the existing national school systems, but that of ensuring that immigrant Turks and others would have an adequate educational background to be able to compete and succeed in the government schools. Thus, in many parts of Western Europe, the Gülen community in its educational efforts has focused on weekend classes and tutorials aimed at supplementing the instruction given in the state schools and at preparing for standardized exams.

In the schools associated with the movement in the United States, mainly located in areas with a high concentration of Turkish-Americans, the challenge has been to provide an opportunity for students to attain a high level of academic achievement. In fact, particularly in scientific fields, in regions such as New Jersey and Texas, schools run by members of the Hizmet Movement have been among the most highly awarded schools in the state. These schools are not "Islamic schools" in that even though the inspiration for the schools is found in enlightened Islamic ideals, both the teaching and administrative staff and the student body are made up of the followers of other religions as well as of Muslims. In some cases, religious instruction is offered once a week, while in other cases religion is not taught in the schools.

The schools do not form a centralized "school system." Each is established and run by individual members of the Gülen community in a privately registered and funded foundation. The teachers receive a common spiritual training and are sent to where the need is considered the greatest, but there is no central governing board that sends out instructions on educational policy, curriculum, or discipline. Rather, each school is "twinned" with a particular city or region in Turkey, where businessmen sympathetic to the movement undertake financial responsibility for the new school.

Gülen's genius does not lie so much in reinterpreting the teaching of the Qur'an as in applying traditional Islamic prescriptions in entirely new ways to respond to constantly changing social needs. According to the Albanian scholar Bekim Agai:

"The key point for Gülen is that the Islamic principles are unchanging, yet must be given concrete form in each new era. Once, a Qur'an course might have been the best way to invest Islamic donations, but [today] other Islamic activities take precedence. He succeeds in gaining support in conservative Islamic circles for new Islamic fields of action by using traditional Islamic terminology and defining his terms conventionally, but at the same time furnishing them with innovative implications for the present day. He argues that questions of morality and education are more essential for today's Islam than political issues, and that present-day Muslims are confronted with entirely different problems than the question of whether or not to introduce the *sharia*."

Commitment to Dialogue

The community inherited its commitment to interreligious dialogue and cooperation from the writings of Said Nursi, but this commitment has been renewed and given new impetus in the writings of Fethullah Gülen. In his speech in 1999 at the Parliament of the World's Religions in Capetown, Gülen presented an optimistic vision of interreligious harmony: "It is my conviction that in the future years, the new millennium will witness unprecedented religious blooming and the followers of world religions, such as Muslims, Christians, Jews, Buddhists, Hindus and others, will walk hand-in-hand to build a promised bright future of the world."

Already beginning in 1911 and repeatedly down to his death in 1963, Said Nursi called for "Muslim-Christian unity" to oppose godless tendencies in modern societies. While endorsing Nursi's appeal, Gülen goes beyond Nursi's view in two important respects. Firstly, dialogue and unity is not limited to "the good Christians," as Nursi had proposed, but is now to be extended to the conscientious followers of all religions. The prominent presence and active participation of Jewish as well as Christian representatives at the Abrahamic symposia sponsored by the movement and held in the Turkish cities of Urfa, İstanbul, and Mardin show that the movement is serious in its readiness to dialogue and cooperate with all believers. Secondly, the motivation for this dialogue is not simply a strategic alliance to oppose atheistic and secularizing tendencies in modern life, as Nursi had held, but is called for by the nature of Islamic belief itself.

> The goal of dialogue among world religions is not simply to destroy scientific materialism and the materialistic world view that has caused such harm. Rather, the very nature of religion demands this dialogue. Judaism, Christianity, and Islam, and even Hinduism and Buddhism pursue the same goal. As a Muslim, I accept all Prophets and Books sent to different peoples throughout history, and regard belief in them as an essential principle of being Muslim.[121]

To further its pursuits of interreligious dialogue, the Hizmet Movement has created the Intercultural Dialogue Platform as a project of the movement's İstanbul-based Writers and Journalists Foundation. The IDP has been particularly active in sponsoring and organizing "Abrahamic" dialogues with high-ranking representatives of Judaism, Christianity, and Islam. The Hizmet Movement also organizes associations for the promotion of interreli-

---

[121] Fethullah Gülen, Capetown, 1999, p. 14.

gious and intercultural activities at the local and regional level, such as the Cosmicus Foundation in the Netherlands, the Australian Intercultural Society in Melbourne, the Friede-Institut für Dialog in Vienna, the Interfaith Dialog Center of Patterson, New Jersey, Houston's Institute of Interfaith Dialog, and the Niagara Foundation of Chicago, all of which take independent initiatives toward promoting interreligious understanding and cooperation.

I will conclude by illustrating Gülen's method of interpreting Islam by returning to the controversial global issue with which I began, the reaction of Muslims to the cartoons published in the Danish newspaper. Like all Muslims, Gülen was insulted and hurt by the scurrilous caricatures of Muhammad, a sentiment that I think that any serious follower of a religious faith would readily understand. As a Christian in the Catholic tradition, I would certainly be deeply offended by any abusive or disrespectful images of Jesus or his mother.

But what interests us here is Gülen's response to what must have been for him a painful affront and the guidance he offered to the hundreds of thousands of Muslims who look to him for advice and inspiration. In an online interview with a Turkish newspaper ("Cartoon Spite and Our Attitude," en.fgulen.com/pressroom/news/2179-cartoon-spite-and-our-attitude), he notes that Muslims must respond in a civilized manner. There are those in the world who are intolerant of others and who ridicule their beliefs. He continues: "You are by no means allowed to behave in the same way as they did. Their disrespect toward our Prophet is discourteous....but retaliation in kind is never a possibility for you. You can never use those weapons."

He goes on to say that if a Muslim were to speak unfavorably about Jesus, Moses or any other prophet, that Muslim would "take a step away from faith." "The slightest disrespect that you may utter might deprive you of your faith and put a distance between you and God." Muslims, he says, are even forbidden to curse the gods of others, as that would incite the worshipers of that deity to curse the God of Islam, and the Muslim who began the exchange of insults would thereby be responsible for causing the others' blasphemy against God.

What Muslims should do, he says, is to consider how they might positively overcome the situation. "Cursing in return for a curse, burning flags, and hurling insults do not solve the problem. Such reactions will increase the violence and hatred on the other side. What does burning their flag achieve? Such actions are not retaliation in kind, nor are they wise. You only exhibit your feelings of revenge and hatred which further increases the others' hatred." Instead, Gülen calls for civilized action and remaining calm, citing the *hadith* from Muhammad: "Evil must be warded off with what is good and kind."

It is interesting to note that Gülen's view of freedom of expression, in fact, comes very close to the statement issued by the Vatican in regard to the cartoons: "The right to freedom of thought and expression," it said, "cannot imply the right to offend the religious sentiment of believers." (Vatican Press Office, 5 February 2006). "Equally deplorable," the statement added, are the violent reactions of protest." In short, Gülen and the Papal agency have arrived independently at what is a very similar position, that claims to freedom of expression do not justify insulting the faith of others, and that violence is not a proper religious response even to a genuine insult. It is worth reflecting that both arrive at this conclusion not through human rights discourse, but rather through a faith-based ethical discourse: what should believers do, how should they react to wrongs, what is their role in a world filled with much intolerance?

I personally feel encouraged by the advice of leaders like Fethullah Gülen and by the initiatives taken by members of the movement associated with his name. I feel they offer, not only to Muslims, but to secular society itself a high-minded and visionary alternative to violence and reprisal. I wish them success.

Bibliography

David Tittensor, *The House of Service: The Gülen Movement and Islam's Third Way*, New York: Oxford University Press, 2014.

Erkan Acar, *Educating Globally: Case Study of a Gülen-Inspired School in the United States*, New Jersey: Tughra Books, 2014.

Greg Barton, Paul Weller and İhsan Yılmaz, *The Muslim World and Politics in Transition: Creative Contributions of the Gülen Movement*, New York: Bloomsbury Academic, 2013.

Erkan M. Kurt, *So That Others May Live: A Fethullah Gülen Reader*, New York: Blue Dome Press, 2013.

Ori Z. Soltes, *Embracing the World: Fethullah Gülen's Thought and Its Relationship with Jelaluddin Rumi and Others*, New Jersey: Tughra Books, 2013.

Walter Wagner, *Beginnings and Endings: Fethullah Gülen's Vision for Today's World*, New York: Blue Dome Press, 2013.

Tom Gage, *Gülen's Dialogue on Education*, Seattle: Cune, 2013.

M. Hakan Yavuz, Toward an Islamic Enlightenment: The Gülen Movement, Oxford University Press, 2013.

Sophia Pandya and Nancy Gallagher, *The Gülen Hizmet Movement and Its Transnational Activities: Case Studies of Altruistic Activism in Contemporary Islam*, Boca Raton, FL: Brown Walker Press, 2012.

Tamer Balcı and Christopher L. Miller, *The Gülen Hizmet Movement: Circumspect Activism in Faith-Based Reform*, Newcastle upon Tyne, UK: Cambridge Scholars Publishing, 2012.

Martha Ann Kirk, *Growing Seeds of Peace: Stories and Images of Service of the Gülen Movement in Southeastern Turkey*, Houston: Gülen Institute, 2012.

Heon Kim and John Raines, *Making Peace in and with the World: The Gülen Movement and Eco-justice*, Newcastle upon Tyne, UK: Cambridge Scholars Publishing, 2012.

Doğan Koç, *Strategic Defamation of Fethullah Gülen*, Lanham, MD: University Press of America, 2012.

Muhammed Çetin, *Hizmet: Questions and Answers on the Hizmet Movement*, New York: Blue Dome Press, 2012.

İhsan Yılmaz and Paul Weller, *European Muslims, Civility and Public Life: Perspectives On and From the Gülen Movement*, London: Continuum, 2012.

Doğu Ergil, *Fethullah Gülen and the Gülen Movement in 100 Questions*, New York: Blue Dome Press, 2012.

Gürkan Çelik, *The Gülen Movement: Building Social Cohesion through Dialogue and Education*, Delft: Eburon, 2011.

James C. Harrington, *Wrestling with Free Speech, Religious Freedom, and Democracy in Turkey: The Political Trials and Times of Fethullah Gülen*, Lanham, MD: University Press of America, 2011.

Maimul Ahsan Khan, *The Vision and Impact of Fethullah Gülen: A New Paradigm for Social Activism*, New York: Blue Dome Press, 2011.

İsmail Albayrak, *Mastering Knowledge in Modern Times: Fethullah Gülen as an Islamic Scholar*, New York: Blue Dome Press, 2011.

Muhammed Çetin, *The Gülen Movement: Civic Service without Borders*, New York: Blue Dome Press, 2010.

John L. Esposito and İhsan Yılmaz, *Islam and Peacebuilding: Gülen Movement Initiatives*, New York: Blue Dome Press, 2010.

Helen Rose Ebaugh, *The Gülen Movement: A Sociological Analysis of a Civic Movement Rooted in Moderate Islam*, Dordrecht: Springer, 2009.

Robert Hunt and Yüksel Aslandoğan, *Muslim Citizens of the Globalized World*, New Jersey: Tughra Books, 2007.

B. Jill Carroll, *A Dialogue of Civilizations*, New Jersey: Tughra Books, 2007.

Nevval Sevindi, Contemporary Islamic Conversations: M. Fethullah Gülen on Turkey, Islam, and the West, New York: State University of New York Press, 2007.

Zeki Sarıtoprak, "Islam in Contemporary Turkey: The Contributions of Fethullah Gülen," *The Muslim World,* Special Issue, Vol. 95, Issue 3, July 2005.

Mehmet Kalyoncu, *A Civilian Response to Ethno-Religious Conflict*, New Jersey: Tughra Books, 2004.

M. Hakan Yavuz and John L. Esposito, *Turkish Islam and the Secular State: The Gülen Movement*, Syracuse: Syracuse University Press, 2003.

Shirin Akiner, "Religion's Gap,"*Harvard International Review*, Winter 2000.

The Economist, "Islamic Evangelists," 6 July 2000.

Mehmet Ali Soydan, *Fethullah Gülen Olayı* [The Case of Fethullah Gülen], İstanbul: Biray, 1999.

Ali Ünal and Mustafa Armağan, *Medya Aynasında Fethullah Gülen* [Fethullah Gülen as Portrayed by the Media], İstanbul: Gazeteciler ve Yazarlar Vakfı Yayınları, 1999.

Elisabeth Özdalga, "Entrepreneurs with a Mission: Turkish Islamists Building Schools along the Silk Road," (paper delivered at the Annual Conference of the North American Middle East Studies Association), 1999.

M. Hakan Yavuz, "Societal Search for a New Contract: Fethullah Gülen, Virtue Party and the Kurds," *SAIS Review* 19/1, Winter/Spring 1999

Bülent Aras "Turkish Islam's Moderate Face," *Middle East Quarterly* 5/3: 25, 1998.

Osman Özsoy, *Fethullah Gülen Hocaefendi ile Mülakat* [An Interview with Fethullah Gülen], İstanbul: Alfa, 1998.

Oral Çalışlar, *Fethullah Gülen'den Cemalettin Kaplan'a* [From Fethullah Gülen to Cemalettin Kaplan], İstanbul: Pencere, 1998.

Eyüp Can, *Fethullah Gülen Hocaefendi ile Ufuk Turu* [A Tour of New Horizons with Fethullah Gülen], İstanbul: Milliyet, 1995.

Works Cited

Atay, Rıfat, "Reviving the *Suffa* Tradition," *Muslim World in Transition: Contributions of the Gülen Movement*, London: Leeds Metropolitan University Press, 2007.

Barton, Greg, "Preaching by Example and Learning for Life: Understanding the Gülen *Hizmet* in the Global Context of Religious Philanthropy and Civil Religion," in *Muslim World in Transition: Contributions of the Gülen Movement*, London: Leeds Metropolitan University Press, 2007.

Benedict XVI, Pope, *Love in Truth (Caritas in Veritate)*, 29 June 2009.

_____ "Address to Members of the 'Centesimus Annus' Foundation," 19 May 2006.

_____ "Address to the Italian Christian Workers' Associations (A.C.L.I.)," 27 January 2006.

_____ "Address to the Representatives of Other Religions," Washington, D.C., 23 April 2008.

Çetin, Muhammed, "Fethullah Gülen and the Contribution of Islamic scholarship to Democracy," *The Fountain*, 4 January 2009.

Gardet, L., *Encyclopaedia of Islam*, Leiden: 2006.

Gökçek, Mustafa, "Fethullah Gülen and Sufism: a Historical Perspective," *Muslim Citizens of the Globalized World: Contributions of the Gülen Movement* (ed. Robert Hunt and A. Yüksel Aslandoğan), New Jersey: The Light, 2007.

Gülen, Fethullah, "A Comparative Approach to Islam and Democracy," *SAIS (School of Advanced International Studies) Review*, 21, 2:2001.

_____ *Advocate of Dialogue*, Fairfax, VA: The Fountain, 2000.

_____ "An Ideal Society," The Fountain, 32, October–December, 2000.

_____ "An Interview with Fethullah Gülen" (translated by Zeki Saritoprak and Ali Unal), *The Muslim World* (Islam in Contemporary Turkey: The Contribution of Fethullah Gülen), 95/3, July 2005.

_____ *Criteria or Lights of the Way*, İzmir: Kaynak, 1998.

_____ "*Ibada, Ubudiya,* and *Ubuda* (Worship, Servanthood, and Deep Devotion)," *The Fountain,* 71, October–November, 2009.

_____ *Key Concepts in the Practice of Sufism,* İzmir: Kaynak, 1997.

_____ *Key Concepts in the Practice of Sufism* (II), Somerset NJ: The Light, 2004.

_____ *Prophet Muhammad as Commander,* İzmir: Kaynak, 1998.

_____ *Prophet Muhammad: the Infinite Light,* İzmir: Kaynak, 1998.

_____ *Questions This Modern Age Puts to Islam,* İzmir: Kaynak, 1998.

_____ "Sufism and Its Origins," *The Fountain,* July–September 1999.

_____ "*Taqwa* (Piety)," *The Fountain,* 69, May–June 2009.

_____ "The Necessity of Interfaith Dialogue: a Muslim Approach," *Parliament of the World's Religions,* Capetown, 1999.

_____ *Toward a Global Civilization of Love and Tolerance,* Somerset, NJ: The Light, 2004.

_____ *Towards the Lost Paradise,* London: Truestar, 1996.

_____ "Towards the World of the Righteous Servants," *The Fountain,* 7, July–September 1994.

_____ "Turkey Assails a Revered Islamic Moderate," *Turkish Daily News,* 25 August 2000.

_____ *Understanding and Belief: the Essentials of Islamic Faith,* İzmir: Kaynak, 1997.

Kamış, Mehmet, "Medeniyetler Buluşması," *Aksiyon,* 14 February 1998.

Kim, Heon, "Gülen's Dialogic Sufism: A Constructional and Constructive Factor of Dialogue," *Islam in the Age of Global Challenges: Alternative Perspectives of the Gülen Movement,* Washington: Rumi Forum, 2008.

Lewis, Bernard, *The Emergence of Modern Turkey,* Oxford: Oxford University Press, 1969.

Michel, Thomas, "Der türkische Islam im Dialog mit der modernen Gesellschaft. Die neo-sufistische Spiritualität der Gülen-Bewegung," *Concilium,* Dezember, 2005.

_____ "Fethullah Gülen as Educator," *Turkish Islam and the Secular State* (ed. M. Hakan Yavuz and John L. Esposito), Syracuse: Syracuse University Press, 2003.

_____ "Sufism and Modernity in the Thought of Fethullah Gülen," *The Muslim World,* 95/3: 2005.

Nursi, Said, *The Letters,* İstanbul: Sözler, 1997.

Özdalga, Elisabeth, "Worldly Asceticism in Islamic Casting: Fethullah Gülen's Inspired Piety and Activism," *Critique*, 17 (Fall 2000).

Saritoprak, Zeki, "Fethullah Gülen: A Sufi in His Own Way," *Turkish Islam and the Secular State* (ed. M. Hakan Yavuz and John L. Esposito), Syracuse: Syracuse University Press, 2003.

Schimmel, Anne-Marie, *Mystical Dimensions of Islam*, Chapel Hill: University of North Carolina Press, 1975.

Webb, Lynne Emily, *Fethullah Gülen: Is There More to Him than Meets the Eye*, Patterson, N.J.: Zinnur Books, 1983.

Yavuz, M. Hakan, "The Gülen Movement: the Turkish Puritans," in *Turkish Islam and the Secular State* (ed. M. Hakan Yavuz and John L. Esposito), Syracuse: Syracuse University Press, 2003.

Yılmaz, İhsan, "Changing Turkish-Muslim Discourses on Modernity, West and Dialogue," paper delivered at the International Association of Middle East Studies (IAMES), Berlin, 5–7 October 2000.

_____ "*Ijtihad* and *Tajdid* by Conduct: The Gülen Movement," *Turkish Islam and the Secular State* (ed. M. Hakan Yavuz and John L. Esposito), Syracuse: Syracuse University Press, 2003.

Index